StyleCity

BARCELONA

With over 350 colour photographs and 6 maps

SALCHICHO

QUESO

CHORIZO

SOBRASAD

TORTILLA PATA

¨ FRAN

ATUN

Contents

Street Wise

Style Traveller

Series concept and editor: Lucas Dietrich
Research and author: Phyllis Richardson
Original design and map concept: The Senate
Jacket and book design: Grade Design Consultants
Maps: Peter Bull

Specially commissioned photography by
Ingrid Rasmussen and Anthony Webb

Although every effort has been made to ensure that the information in this book is as up-to-date and as accurate as possible at the time of going to press, some details are liable to change.

First published in the United Kingdom in 2003 by
Thames & Hudson Ltd, 181A High Holborn,
London WC1V 7QX

www.thamesandhudson.com

Reprinted 2004

British Library Cataloguing-in-Publication Data
A catalogue record for this book is available from the British Library

ISBN 0-500-21008-X

Printed in China

How to Use This Guide

The book features two principal sections: **Street Wise** and **Style Traveller**.

Street Wise, which is arranged by neighbourhood, features areas that can be covered in a day (and night) on foot and includes a variety of locations – cafés, shops, restaurants, museums, performance spaces, bars – that capture local flavour or are lesser-known destinations.

The establishments in the **Style Traveller** section represent the city's best and most characteristic locations – 'worth a detour' – and feature hotels (**sleep**), restaurants (**eat**), cafés and bars (**drink**), boutiques and shops (**shop**) and getaways (**retreat**).

Each location is shown as a circled number on the relevant neighbourhood map, which is intended to provide a rough idea of location and proximity to major sights and landmarks rather than precise position. Locations in each neighbourhood are presented sequentially by map number. Each entry in the **Style Traveller** has two numbers: the top one refers to the page number of the neighbourhood map on which it appears; the second number is its location.

For example, the visitor might begin by selecting a hotel from the **Style Traveller** section. Upon arrival, **Street Wise** might lead him to the best joint for coffee before guiding him to a house-museum nearby. After lunch he might go to find a special jewelry store listed in the **shop** section. For a memorable dining experience, he might consult his neighbourhood section to find the nearest restaurant crossreferenced to **eat** in **Style Traveller**.

Street addresses are given in each entry, and complete information – including email and web addresses – is listed in the alphabetical **contact** section. Travel and contact details for the destinations in **retreat** are given at the end of **contact**.

Note that all street names are given in Catalan, though some taxi drivers, street signs, restaurants and locals still use Castilian Spanish.

Legend

(2) Location

Museums, sights

Gardens, squares

(M) Subway stops

Streets

BARCELONA

Barcelona boasts a unique heritage of cultural achievement, political and military independence and artistic refinement. It is a regional (Catalan) rather than national or international capital city like Paris or London, and yet its smaller size seems to crystallize its many attributes into a brilliant urban gem: compact, accessible, coastal, with historic quarters, as well as substantial renovated sections that are tourist-friendly without being blandly overcommercialized. Much of its newfound popularity has been gained with the high-profile projects completed in association with its hosting the summer Olympics of 1992. The Olympic stadium and Santiago Calatrava's poetic telecommunications tower exclaiming rather than marring the hillside landscape in Montjuïc were just the beginning. The cleaning up of beaches, the building of the Olympic Village and Port (to designs by Bohigas, Martorell and Mackay) and rehabilitation of Port Vell with the new aquarium, IMAX theatre and connecting walkways, bridges and clusters of restaurants reclaimed and revealed a stunning shoreline for public enjoyment. The programme of improvements continues and brings with it a new artistic and cultural flowering.

Despite the developments around the waterfront, visitors are drawn to the Ciutat Vella, the 'old city' that encompasses the area around the Catedral and the rest of the Barri Gòtic, the Ribera, Barceloneta and the Raval, each with its distinctive feel. The Barri Gòtic is a medieval quarter of narrow passages, studded wood doors, massive low arches and grand stone palaces. The Ribera, too, exudes Gothic enchantment and has the city's first designed street, Carrer de Montcada. The Ribera, once an run-down quarter near the harbour, is today home to the crackling nightlife of El Born. The area known as the Raval, which was for centuries beyond the pale, was claimed first by the monasteries and then by the overflowing population. For generations it was a gritty haven for outsiders; now it is evolving into an edgy artistic quarter.

Large-scale development plans began long before the Olympic bid. It was in the 19th century that the area to the north of and surrounding the Ciutat Vella was laid out as a meticulously planned residential and commercial zone – the Eixample, or 'enlargement' – by the civic engineer Ildefons Cerdà. However, what this planning facilitated was not just the spread of the population and its businesses, but a grander civic statement – the imperial-style thoroughfare of Passeig de Gràcia – as well as the development of the works of the Modernista movement, Catalunya's unique version of Art Nouveau. Here the young Antoni Gaudí accomplished some of his most significant works, with the Sagrada Familia hovering unfinished north of the Diagonal. But Gaudí was just one exponent of this remarkable style. Lluís Domènech i Montaner and Josep Puig i Cadafalch also created world-masterworks in the wake of Eixample development. Some Modernista buildings suffered the vagaries of fashion and some were even lost, but the Barcelonans have long since recognized the genius of their native sons to the extent that there is a movement at present to have their most famous builder, Gaudí, canonized. In later years, the vanguard architectural tradition has stayed at the international limelight through such architects as Josep Lluís Sert, Oscar Tusquets and Ricardo Bofill.

Northwest of the Eixample, the former villages of Gràcia, Bonanova and Horta and the Zona Alta, once at the periphery of the city, have a relaxed atmosphere that is charged with the creative urban flair of Barcelona. But it is a flair grown partly from hardship. This city, like its other European counterparts, has been marked by wars, most notably the Spanish Civil War (1936–39). In the aftermath of their resistance, the Catalan language was outlawed and only reinstated, rigorously, after Franco's death in 1975. Barcelona is now a bilingual city where Castillian is spoken alongside Catalan and signs appear in either Catalan or both languages.

From the tiny streets of the Ciutat Vella to the wide Eixample and beyond it is evident that the city's aesthetic achievement (*disseny*, or 'design') is a serious pursuit, a force that has been sharply honed through recent decades. So much so, in fact, that the Royal Institute of British Architects, who usually bestow their annual Royal Gold Medal to an architect, named all of Barcelona worthy of the accolade in 1999. Meanwhile, contemporary designers of furniture (Jaume Tresserra), objects (Javier Mariscal) and fashion (Antonio Miró) have achieved international renown but are the tip of the iceberg in a place where new talent is on show everywhere, from small galleries and showroom-shop-ateliers to street and clubwear designers with global followings. New and fantastically designed bars have emerged to cater to the design-conscious youth, and Catalan chefs are challenging the culinary giants of the past to put Catalan cuisine firmly on the gastronomic destination map. This small creative centre, which counts modern masters Picasso, Miró and Tàpies among its best-known cultural exports and which has stood for centuries of independence, exudes a spirit of optimism, modernity and innovation that shines from the depths of the Barri Gòtic to the heights of Tibidabo.

Street Wise

Catedral • Barri Gòtic • La Ribera • Barceloneta •
Poble Nou • El Raval • Montjuïc • Eixample •
Gràcia • Zona Alta

Catedral

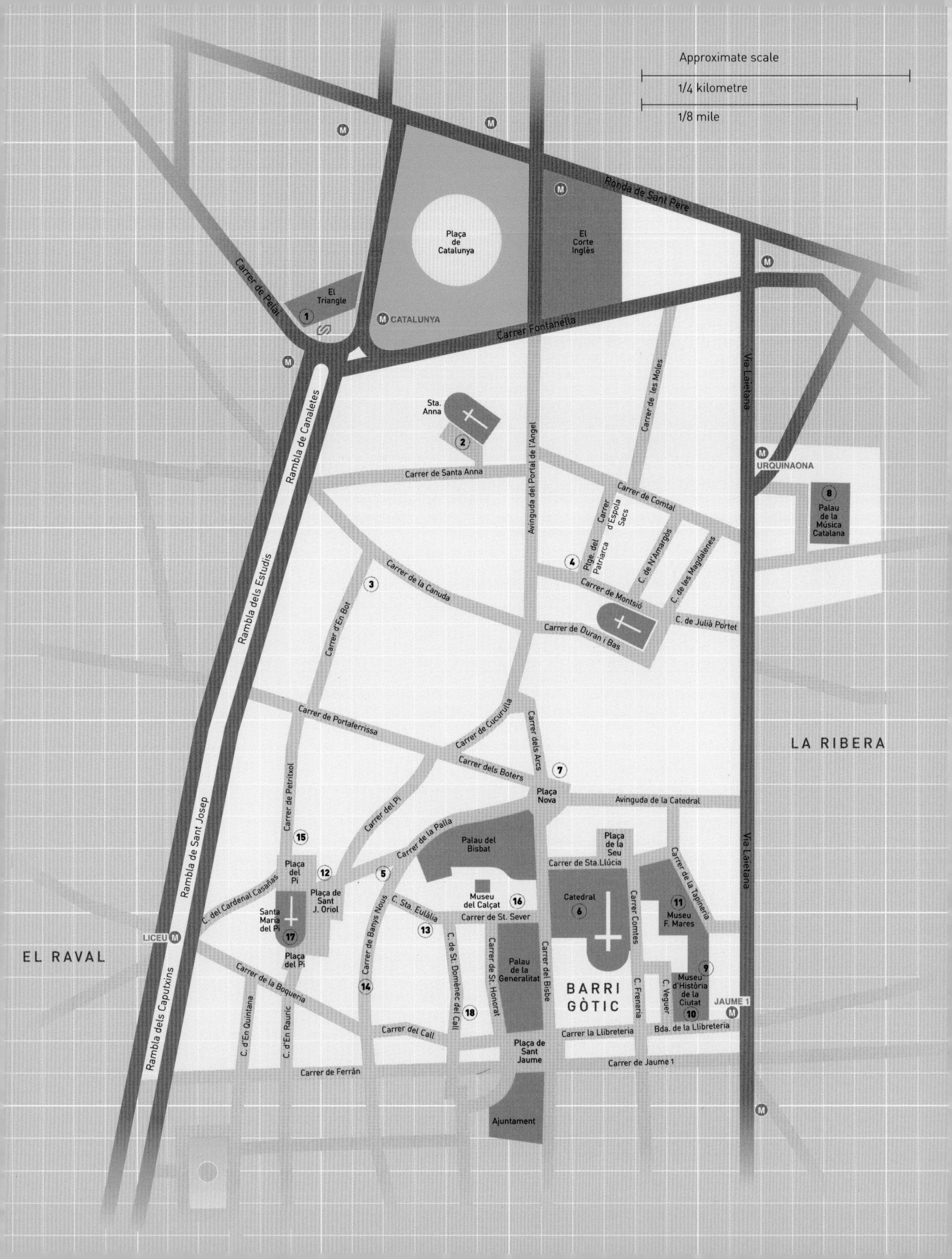

Approximate scale
1/4 kilometre
1/8 mile
Ronda de Sant Pere
Plaça de Catalunya
El Corte Inglès
Carrer de Pelai
El Triangle
CATALUNYA
Carrer Fontanella
Via Laietana
Carrer de les Moles
Sta. Anna
Rambla de Canaletes
Avinguda del Portal de l'Angel
URQUINAONA
Carrer de Santa Anna
Carrer de Comtal
Palau de la Música Catalana
Carrer d'Espola Sacs
Ptge. del Patriarca
C. de N'Amargós
C. de les Magdalenes
Carrer de la Canuda
Carrer de Montsió
Rambla dels Estudis
Carrer d'En Bot
C. de Julià Portet
Carrer de Duran i Bas
Carrer de Portaferrissa
Carrer de Cucurulla
Carrer dels Arcs
LA RIBERA
Carrer dels Boters
Carrer de Petritxol
Plaça Nova
Avinguda de la Catedral
Rambla de Sant Josep
Carrer del Pi
Carrer de la Palla
Palau del Bisbat
Plaça de la Seu
Plaça del Pi
Carrer de Sta.Llúcia
Carrer de la Tapineria
Via Laietana
C. del Cardenal Casañas
Plaça de Sant J. Oriol
Museu del Calçat
Catedral
C. Sta. Eulàlia
Carrer de St. Sever
Museu F. Mares
Santa Maria del Pi
Carrer Comtes
LICEU
Plaça del Pi
Carrer de Banys Nous
C. de St. Domènec del Call
Carrer de St. Honorat
Palau de la Generalitat
Carrer del Bisbe
EL RAVAL
Carrer de la Boqueria
BARRI GÒTIC
C. Freneria
C. Veguer
Museu d'Història de la Ciutat
JAUME 1
Rambla dels Caputxins
C. d'En Quintana
C. d'En Rauric
Carrer del Call
Plaça de Sant Jaume
Carrer la Llibreteria
Bda. de la Llibreteria
Carrer de Jaume 1
Carrer de Ferrán
Ajuntament

Barcelona's ancient and medieval histories come together in the northwestern corner of the Barri Gòtic, where the cathedral, begun in 1298, sits next to the 2nd-3rd–century Roman walls and ruins of the Temple of Augustus, still recognizable enough to make the past alive. The church that is dearest to Barcelonans is Santa Maria del Mar (p. 45), which is partly due to the fact that the cathedral' s construction, started around the same time, was not completed until the early 20th century. Still, flanked by wide plazas, the cathedral commands an authority over the city. Away from the modernized shopping precinct of the Portal de l'Angel the neighbourhood reflects this tie to the city's early origins, as the concentration of old shops in the small surrounding streets selling antiques, trinkets and religious artefacts attests. The modern architects' cooperative is also close by here, adding an element of cutting-edge modernity to the hallowed old setting, as is Els Quatre Gats (p. 16) , one of Barcelona's best-loved turn-of-the-century bohemian cafés.

The historic centre is also home to centuries-old palaces that have gone through stages of splendour, neglect and refurbishment but still hold themselves with the firm grace and dignity for which the Catalans have long been known. Many have been painstakingly restored, but for the most part are not held in rarefied quarantine and are open to the public. The Palau del Rei, for example, is now home to the Museu d'Història de la Ciutat and gives access to more of the city's Roman foundations. The palace, once a royal residence, defines a fine medieval plaza and contains an outstanding Gothic salon, probably the setting for Columbus's reception by the King and Queen of Spain after his first return from the New World.

Jumping across the Via Laietana, the Plaça Lluís Millet brings us to another century and another sort of splendour, Lluís Domènech i Montaner's Palau de la Música Catalana (p. 21), a Modernista extravaganza set in ceramic tiles over stone, iron and glass. Heading west from the cathedral via more narrow streets, you encounter the cosy and intriguing Banys Nous, where antiques shops are clustered together, with enchanting piles of bric-a-brac visible through glass panes, others well-polished and professionally conserved items of serious age, provenance and collecting interest. Farther west is the hulking form of Santa Maria del Pi, another fine representation of Catalan Gothic style that presides over the delightful shady Plaças del Pi and Sant Josep Oriol.

UNMARKING TIME

1 Grus Watch

El Triangle, Carrer de Pelai, 39

Just inside the door of the looming Triangle mall across the Plaça de Catalunya from the massive El Corte Inglés, Grus Watch is a tiny pocket of a design statement that puts these commercial giants to shame. Started in 1991, Grus is a company of Catalan designers who make elegant, minimal watches without any name or trademark marring their pristine forms. There are about 150 of their own watches and a few by other makers on display in this singular outlet and while their style tends towards the spare, there is ample variation in materials, shape and colour. They have earned themselves a high reputation in international design circles and their concept – attention to product detail rather than name recognition – deserves to continue to radiate.

A HIDDEN SANCTUARY

2 Monestir i església de Santa Anna

Carrer de Santa Anna, 27–29

Behind the noisy shopping district of Portal de l'Angel, the church of Santa Anna exists in separate tranquillity through a small stone archway off the Carrer de Santa Anna, where just inside the stone-paved courtyard a little flower stall marks the transition from the commercial zone. The courtyard itself offers quiet respite from the throngs close by but remains almost miraculously insulated from them. Much of the church's 12th- and 14th-century character survives, even though some elements, like the dome, were reconstructed after Civil War bombing. Through the church you can enter the fine cloisters, which were part of the monastery buildings added in the 15th century.

CHOCOLATE FANTASY

3 Xocoa

COOL FOR CATS

4 Els Quatre Gats

Carrer de Montsío, 3 bis

Located in the Casa Martí designed by the Modernista architect Josep Puig i Cadafalch, the Quatre Gats would be a landmark without its storied past, but because of both, it is one of Barcelona's most famous restaurants. Opened in 1897 by Pere Romeu who modelled it after Le Chat Noir in Paris, the Quatre Gats was immediately populated with, and supported by, some of the most important artists of the period, Santiago Rusiñol and Ramon Casas, who helped finance it, and Picasso, who held one of his early exhibitions there and allowed Romeu to use one of his designs for the menu cover. The place closed because of debts in 1903 and suffered a less than dignified existence until the late 1970s. In 1989 the building was restored and the restaurant began to retrieve some of its former bohemian glory. Today it overflows with character, artistic ambience and a good deal of bonhomie.

MONASTERY MADE

5 Caelum

SACRED HEART

6 Catedral de Barcelona

Plaça de la Seu

The cathedral of Barcelona was begun in the 13th century but unlike the more popular and significant Santa Maria del Mar and del Pi, it was not finished for centuries. The façade is in fact early 20th century, and adds a note of modernity to the Ciutat Vella as it is often used to denote the heart of the city. The most interesting aspects are the cloisters with captive white geese, a holdover from Roman occupation, and palm trees.

CENTRE FOR ARCHITECTS

7 Cooperativa d'Arquitectes

Plaça Nova, 5

On the main plaça outside the Cathedral, the 1960s wedge-shaped glass building stands out with a projecting frieze decorated with *sgraffiti* taken from drawings by Picasso. It houses the offices of the architects' cooperative in the tower, while the public exhibition space and the city's main architecture bookshop are located on the ground and lower-ground floors. The bookshop is a must for architecture fiends, stocking not only the necessary titles in architecture, urban design, art and interiors in various languages, but also magazines and tools for drawing, graphics and CAD equipment. They offer discounts to members and to some foreign organizations, so you might as well ask.

ADA EL 1761
BAR DEL PI

SYMPHONIC STRUCTURE

8 Palau de la Música Catalana

Carrer de Sant Françesc de Paula, 2

This Modernista masterpiece designed by luminary architect Lluís Domènech i Montaner (1908) and extended by Oscar Tusquets and Carles Díaz (1983, 2001), reflects the sense of grandeur of the city's late-19th-century development. More than just a venue for Catalan music, it is a riotous celebration of art and was declared a UNESCO World Heritage Site in 1997. The curvaceous red-brick façade animated with busts of Bach, Beethoven and Palestrina, as well as figures from Catalan folklore, and with columns covered in colourfully detailed mosaics, signals the architect's attention to highly ornamental and precise decorative work. Inside the splendours multiply to a breathtaking degree, with grand sweeping staircases carved with classical motifs, vivid tile work and gilt, stamped ceilings. Low, ample columns sprout vast stretches of ribbed vaulting in the tradition of Catalan Gothic, but are topped with whimsical rosette decorations. The stained-glass dome is simply awe-inspiring, and the programme of classical and folk music attracts over half a million visitors a year.

OLD WORLD REVISITED

9 Plaça del Rei and Museu d'Història de la Ciutat

Plaça del Rei, 1

The square enclosed by the palace built during the reign of Pere (Peter) III to house the old counts of Barcelona in the 14th century is a splendid microcosm of Barcelona architecture and history from the 1st to the 16th centuries. The near-perfect medieval façades and the grand stairs leading to the Saló de Tinell, reputedly the site of Columbus's reception by King Ferdinand and Queen Isabella on his first return from the New World, can be appreciated from the outside. Entering the museum gives you access to the Palau interiors, including the wonderful Saló, probably the finest example of secular Catalan Gothic architecture in existence. In one corner of the square is the small, elegant Capella Palatina or Santa Àgata (1319), which was built on the old Roman wall, and the tower named for Martí the Humanist, added in the 16th century. Beneath the well-preserved plaça is an exhibition of in-situ Roman foundations. The plaça can also be enjoyed during outdoor concerts, particularly during the Festival del Grec in the summer.

AN OLD-FASHIONED LIGHT

10 Subirà Cereria

Baixada de la Llibreteria, 7

It is thought to be Barcelona's oldest shop, dating from 1761, as is painted clearly on the front, and moved to this location in the 19th century. However, even without those details, this candle shop near the Cathedral seems to have sprung from a different era. The pale blue-and-white panelling and woodwork full of fanciful Baroque elements, the voluptuous neoclassical female torchères and the pale pink draperies are softly evocative. Don't expect anything psychedelic here; rather fat church candles and tall, elegant spiralling tapers in an array of pale solid colours are sitting prettily on wooden shelves.

ECLECTIC COLLECTION

11 Museu Frederic Marès

Plaça de Sant Iu, 5–6

This intriguing museum, set in a part of the royal palace that was home to bishops in the 13th century and later to members of court and religious orders, shows the collection of Frederic Marès, who lived in an apartment in the building in the 1940s. Though he made his name as a sculptor, his enduring legacy is his highly eclectic collection, which he acquired over his long life and which began with his fascination with religious art and artefacts and grew to encompass a wide range of objects and art. Among the treasures, which include everything from children's toys to postcards, ceramics and daguerreotypes, are some very fine Romanesque and Gothic pieces. There is also ancient and medieval sculpture and rooms dedicated to timepieces, smoking paraphernalia, seashells and wrought-iron work. A café is open from April to September.

HISTORIC BEGINNINGS

12 Bar del Pi

Plaça de Sant Josep Oriol, 1

An institution of the Barri Gòtic, the Bar del Pi saw the founding of the anti-Fascist PSUC in the heady Civil War year of 1936. Today it's as popular as ever and the small interior is easily packed out. There are tables outside, however, especially appealing during the weekends when the art market sets up in the square shaded by the eponymous pine and plane trees, near Santa Maria del Pi (see p. 22). Other days it's a buskers' haven, with varying degrees of talent serenading your drinks and tapas. Inside the bar a piano awaits anyone with a musical inclination.

ANTIQUE TECHNOLOGY

13 Anamorfosis

Carrer Santa Eulalia, 4

Vintage radios, telephones from 1900 to 1950, an 1895 phonograph, 1910 gramophone and lots of other aged gadgets are crowded into the tiny but pristine ordered premises of Anam or fosis. Anna, who must surely corner the market here in scientific, optical and audio antiques, has assembled a collection that encompasses a micro-history of technology. Each piece is immaculate, operable and has been personally selected by Anna herself. Even if you don't have in mind a camerograph from 1906, a vintage typewriter or stacks of vinyl 78 recordings, go for the history lesson.

THE GOOD OLD DAYS

14 Banys Nous Antiques

- Gemma Povo, nos 5–7
- Antigüedades, no. 17A
- L'Arca de l'Àvia, no. 20

Antiques shops have proliferated in the cathedral neighbourhood and a good mix of high-end and bric-a-brac with some rather exceptional specialty shops flourishes along Carrer de Banys Nous. Shops like the generically named Antigüedades, which is stacked to the ceiling with furniture, crockery, the odd painting and knick-knacks, exist happily alongside immaculate collections like that at Gemma Povo. She is the third-generation owner of the family antiquarian shop which is now stocked with Povo's own ironwork lamp and furniture designs alongside a selection of antique Spanish furnishings and objects. Antiques of a different sort are at L'Arca de l'Àvia ('granny's trunk' or 'hope chest'), a lace-draped, charmingly old-fashioned-looking shop that carries clothing and textiles from the 18th and 19th centuries, from delicate lace cloths and shifts to complete formal, embroidered men's suits and wedding dresses. Owner Carmina Viñas had the idea of collecting 'the kinds of things women put in their wedding chests in the 19th century' but her shop has attracted customers beyond the sentimental; her collection is a source for theatre costumes, and she recently found that a number of 19th-century items purchased by an enthusiastic American woman showed up in the film *Titanic*. Viñas also creates her own embroidered textiles based on antique patterns.

SWEET SENSATIONS

15 Granja Dulcinea

148

ONE-WOMAN SHOW

16 La Marthe

Carrer de Sant Sever, 1

Marta Esteban claims an old-fashioned approach to design, though her clothes are anything but retrograde. The shape-hugging designs are made from generous amounts of exceptional fabric and she operates like a mini-haute-couture house, doing about 30 pieces in each collection, exclusively one-offs and made-to-measure articles. For something truly tailormade with a slightly 1940s figure-clinging flavour, ring at no. 1.

SOLEMN AUSTERITY

17 Església Santa Maria del Pi

Plaça del Pi, Plaça de Sant Josep Oriol

Begun in 1322, around the same time as the Santa Maria del Mar, the church of Santa Maria del Pi ('of the pine') was also built in exemplary Catalan Gothic but without the side aisles; only the nave gives access to the wide interior and its 14 chapels. It is a style referred to as 'wide Gothic', which was quite particular to the region and unlike the soaring cathedrals found elsewhere in Europe. As in the Santa Maria del Mar (see p. 45), the interior has a beautiful rose window and other small stained-glass openings that leave the space only dimly lit but extremely atmospheric, although the austerity is more than offset by the brightly painted chapel figures and rather brash-looking modern organ.

TEA BAR EXOTICA

18 Salterio

Carrer Sant Domènec del Call, 4

An intimate, cavernous space with rustic stone walls, low lighting and a few nice Arab touches, Salterio is a bar/tearoom, in a style of drinking spot that has become popular in Barcelona (see also Tetería Jazmín, p. 100) in the last few years. With all the hallmarks of a comfy, convivial bar and all the regular alcoholic and soft drinks available, there is also a wide range of tea served here, not as an afterthought but as a beverage of choice. As well as fruit teas, herbal infusions and the standard Earl Grey or Darjeeling, they also offer Arab-style mint tea and a few more exotic blends, all in an atmosphere that's much groovier than the tea parlour your grandmother might have frequented.

Chicago
llinger
AFICANTE EN COCAINA
KRAUS
las locas
EL HOMBRE LEON
STUDIOS ANATOMICOS
Fenómenos · Galería de
Arte · Historia natural
LO

Barri Gòtic

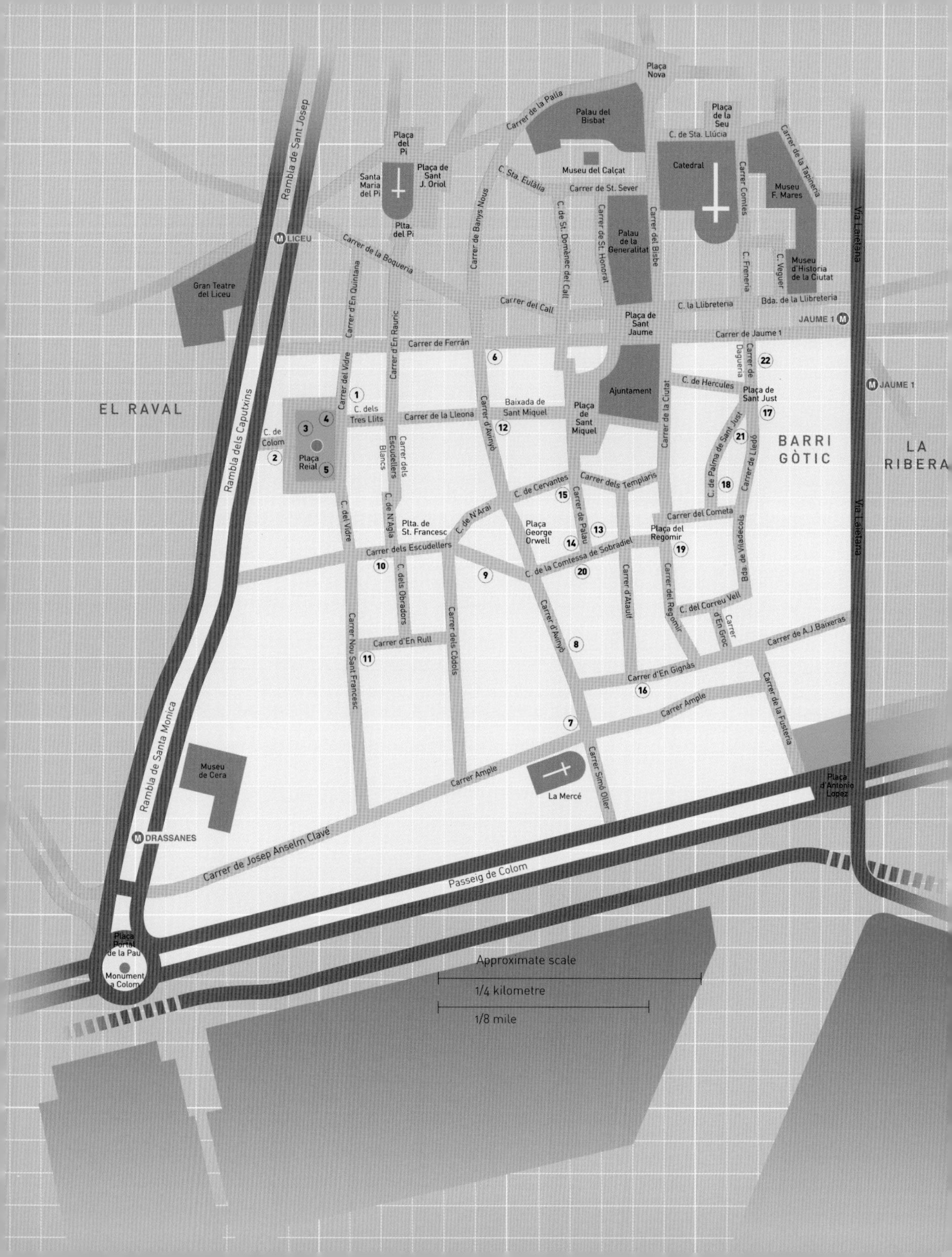

Plaça Nova
Carrer de la Palla
Palau del Bisbat
Plaça de la Seu
C. de Sta. Llúcia
Catedral
Carrer de la Tapineria
Plaça del Pi
Plaça de Sant J. Oriol
Santa Maria del Pi
Museu del Calçat
C. Sta. Eulàlia
Carrer de St. Sever
Carrer Comtes
Museu F. Mares
Rambla de Sant Josep
Plta. del Pi
Carrer de Banys Nous
C. de St. Domènec del Call
Carrer de St. Honorat
Palau de la Generalitat
Carrer del Bisbe
Via Laietana
LICEU
Carrer de la Boqueria
C. Freneria
C. Veguer
Museu d'Historia de la Ciutat
Gran Teatre del Liceu
Carrer d'En Quintana
Carrer del Call
Plaça de Sant Jaume
C. la Llibreteria
Bda. de la Llibreteria
JAUME 1
Carrer d'En Rauric
Carrer de Ferrán
Carrer de Jaume 1
Carrer de Daguería
Carrer del Vidre
C. de Hercules
Ajuntament
Plaça de Sant Just
EL RAVAL
C. dels Tres Llits
Carrer de la Lleona
Baixada de Sant Miquel
Plaça de Sant Miquel
Carrer d'Avinyó
Carrer de la Ciutat
C. de Palma de Sant Just
Carrer de Lledó
BARRI GÒTIC
LA RIBERA
C. de Colom
Plaça Reial
Carrer dels Escudellers Blancs
Rambla dels Caputxins
C. de Cervantes
Carrer dels Templaris
C. del Vidre
C. de N'Aglá
Plta. de St. Francesc
C. de N'Arai
Plaça George Orwell
Carrer de Palau
Carrer del Cometa
Plaça del Regomir
Bda. de Viladecols
Carrer dels Escudellers
C. de la Comtessa de Sobradiel
C. dels Obradors
Carrer d'Ataulf
Carrer del Regomir
C. del Correu Vell
Carrer d'En Groc
Carrer Nou Sant Francesc
Carrer dels Còdols
Carrer d'En Rull
Carrer de A.J.Baixeras
Carrer d'En Gignàs
Carrer de la Fusteria
Carrer Ample
Rambla de Santa Monica
Museu de Cera
La Mercé
Carrer Simó Oller
Plaça d'Antonio Lopez
DRASSANES
Carrer de Josep Anselm Clavé
Passeig de Colom
Plaça Portal de la Pau
Monument a Colom
1 2 3 4 5 6 7 8 9 10 11 12 13 14 15 16 17 18 19 20 21 22
Approximate scale
1/4 kilometre
1/8 mile

South of the cathedral and below Carrer de Ferran–Carrer de Jaume I is the Barri Gòtic's real medieval heart, with narrow streets lined with giant wood doors and sculpted façades leaning this way and that. The Plaça de Sant Jaume, the site of the Roman forum, marks the official beginnings of the medieval city, being flanked by two of the Barcelona's most important symbols of Catalan self-rule: the Casa de la Ciutat, begun in 1373, and the Palau de la Generalitat (1418–1596), enduring symbols that anchor the neighbourhood's medieval and modern character. The Plaça Reial (p. 30) brings the neighbourhood forward to the 19th century, when it was designed as a unified piece and decorated with lamp posts by Antoni Gaudí. The elegant, neoclassical façades with palm tree sentinels have long served as a backdrop to some of the city's less desirable activities, while in a classic urban mix of gritty and chic it attracts a puzzlingly steady stream of tourists and locals, since its restoration in the 1980s by Federico Correa and Alfons Milà, who were also responsible for two of the city's most groundbreaking 1970s interiors.

The Barri Gòtic conjures almost surreal images of shadowy stone walkways, overlooked by picturesque shuttered windows and viewed through planted balconies and washing lines. Remarkably clear of detritus and preserved almost too perfectly, these streets have an air of enchantment about them and might seem like a Disneyfied version of a historic city if it weren't for the evidence of everyday life streaming by and the voices floating through the corridors. The city's, and possibly the world's most famous maker of espadrilles is still in a shop on the Carrer d'Avinyó (p. 164), a street once known for ladies of the night, now the place for young ladies and men to find clothes by breaking young local designers.

Today the Barri Gòtic is settled in its revivified state, less obviously on the rise than El Born (see p. 43), with medieval spaces modernized not just for habitation and shops but to make way for innovative new restaurants and atmospheric cocktail bars. Some spaces have long housed reputable dining rooms serving traditional fare to locals (see Agut or Café de l'Academia, both p. 37). Lately, however, former warehouses, store-houses and wine cellars have been taken over by up-and-coming chefs fusing international tastes and fresh regional produce in chic interiors. Night spots have been decked out in funky Bohemian or futuristic neon and overflow with young people sipping exotic cocktails to vibrant dance music. But the Gothic character prevails, making the step from glowing drinking den or artfully designed nouvelle restaurant into a looming medieval walkway that much more beguiling.

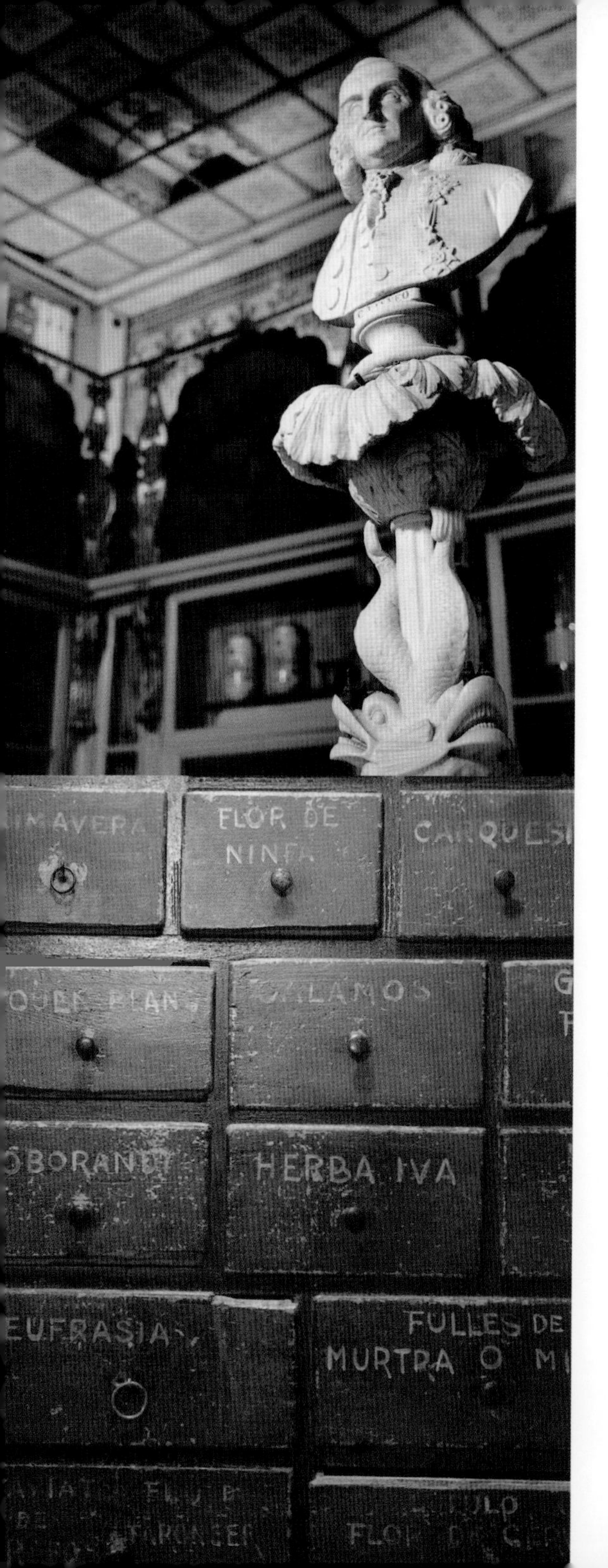

HERBS OF LIFE

1 Herboristeria del Rei

Carrer del Vidre, 1

A little herbal boutique just off of the Plaça Reial, Herboristeria del Rei opened in 1823 and gained the patronage of Isabella II. The old-fashioned corner premises continue to stock a cornucopia of medicinal plants, spices and teas, as well as varieties of honey and other specialized produce. The interior is remarkably quaint, though the fountain and little bath overlooked by a bust of Linnaeus, once used, legend has it, for leeches, might provoke a shiver. Look for the packets of saffron tucked into decorative glass jars, an ideal gift.

JAM SESSIONS

2 Jamboree

Plaça Reial, 17

This ambient cellar jazz club first opened its doors in 1959 and soon became legendary, hosting such luminaries as Ella Fitzgerald, Chet Baker and Lionel Hampton. Then came periods of neglect and closure. The Mas brothers started their career with the highly popular dance club La Boîte (Diagonal, 477) and later added Moog (Arc del Teatre, 3), a techno club that has its own devoted following and reputation for featuring top Spanish and local DJs, in the Raval. The brothers did jazz aficionados a real favour in re-opening Jamboree as a dedicated venue for live jazz and blues, as well as a venue for late-night hip-hop and funk dance music, in 1994. Of an evening, the live acts appear first. New York piano supremo Brad Meldau recorded one of his earliest albums here (with Jordi and Mario Rossy and Perico Sambeat), and recent guests have included Peter King and Danilo Perez, but if you miss out, you might be able to get a recording from the Mas i Mas record label. After the live shows, the place is re-animated with DJs playing a special selection of dance tracks.

POPULAR APPEAL

3 Plaça Reial

During the day, if you can see your way past the many street people, you'll appreciate the architectural achievement of the plaça itself, which was laid out in 1859 by Francesc Daniel Molina (see also La Boqueria market, p. 67) but remodelled in 1981 by Federico Correa and Alfons Milà, who also contributed to the Olympic buildings of Montjuïc, as well as award-winning interiors at Flash-Flash and Giardinetto (both p. 104). The architects transformed the square into a pedestrian zone, conserving the fountain of the Three Graces and the lamps designed by the young Antoni Gaudí amid the graceful pairing of neoclassical façades and mature palm trees, lending the square an atmosphere that is seedy yet lovable and perennially fascinating.

GET STUFFED

4 Taxidermista

Plaça Reial, 8

Architect Beth Galí transformed this former taxidermy shop, which was previously the Museu de Ciències where Salvador Dalí reputedly purchased thousands of dissected ants, into one of the Barri Gòtic's most sought-after dining rooms. Subtle modern interventions and aged industrial elements mix in this newly civilized corner of the Plaça Reial. Outside tables under the shade of the plaça's arcade are a favourite spot for tapas. The dinner menu of chef Miguel Plazaola is a more formal fusion with dishes like tuna with peppers, eggplant and goat's cheese. It also features desserts by Jordi Butrón (see Espai Sucre, p. 138).

SMOKING ROOMS

5 Pipa Club

Plaça Reial, 3

Located in elegant rooms overlooking Plaça Reial, this really is a club for pipe-smoking (and collecting) enthusiasts. But after 11 pm even non-smoking guests are invited to come in for a casual drink, a game of pool and some smoky conversation. Occasionally you can hear live jazz or a DJ. Choose from the gentlemanly Sala Borkum Riff, with its panelled walls, the Games Room, the Dining Room or the Pub Sherlock Holmes. It's ideal for a stop after dinner at Taxidermista (above), though there is also a dining room.

OLD SOFT SHOES

6 La Manual Alpargatera

NEW DESIGNER KNITWEAR

7 Zsu Zsa

Carrer d'Avinyó, 50

Among the many fashion and design boutiques that enliven the Carrer d'Avinyó, some stand out as originals. Zsu Zsa (pronounced Soo-sa) is the name of the designer who produces some really luxuriously soft angora sweaters and other knitwear as well as wide-wale corduroy trousers and jackets. She also turns out nicely tailored blouses and some funkier and flirtier numbers. This is the only shop that sells her own label exclusively, though she shares space with a few other designers in the boutique Suite in Gràcia, Carrer Verdi, 3–5.

STREET FASHION

8 Carrer d'Avinyó

- [Z]INK, no. 14
- Sita Murt, no. 18
- So_Da, no. 24

One of the brothels formerly on this street was supposedly the setting for Picasso's *Les Demoiselles d'Avignon*. Now Carrer d'Avinyó is better known for girls (and boys) of a slightly more style-conscious bent. From the traditional craft of La Manual Alpargatera (see p. 164) Carrer d'Avinyó picks up speed and currency with some of the trendiest shops for street- and clubwear in Barcelona. [Z]INK may be a shop full of Levi's, but it's vintage and Levi's Red that you'll find; the trainers are Adidas Originals and there is an overall Barcelona flavour to the selection, if not the designers themselves. Sita Murt is a truly avant-garde space made to look like an ancient cave, with giant tubular lighting puncturing the stony surfaces and carrying women's fashion by Esteve, Sita Murt and Cultura, as well as Antik Batik, Save the Queen and Pianura. A particularly Barcelona hybrid creation is So_Da, which during the day is a selective boutique in the front featuring mostly clothes by international streetwear designers – Miss Sixty, Boxfresh, Pauric Sweeney, Yohji Yamamoto – all displayed in roll-away cabinets. In the evening, the cabinets are moved aside to give access to the bar in the back, and the whole place is bathed in a seductive red glow. These are a few among many of Avinyó's temptations, so leave yourself time to sample.

FUNKY FANTASTIC

9 Carrer dels Escudellers

- Futura, no. 56
- Harlem Jazz Club, Carrer Comtessa de Sobradiel, 8

It's hard to find a street in the Barri Gòtic that isn't full of interesting little shops, bars and cafés but Escudellers is one with particular appeal. Almost deserted of an afternoon except for the chatter emanating from one of the hippest-looking laundrettes you're ever likely to encounter, on the Placeta de Sant Francesc, it becomes in the evenings a magnet for the new bohemian crowds who wander from one dimly lit destination to another. Fonfone (see p. 157) leads a veritable pack of late-night bars and music-dance venues. A trip to Futura in the afternoon will help prepare for the evening ahead, bringing you both their trendy own-label clothing and CDs to get you in the club-hopping mood. If it's something more sultry you require then head off Escudellers on to Carrer de la Comtessa de Sobradiel and one of the city's favourite jazz venues, the Harlem Jazz Club, where African, Caribbean and blues alternate with the sizzling late-night jazz until 5 am Fridays and Saturdays.

GREEN AND GROOVY

10 Fonfone

HATS THAT TURN HEADS

11 Nina Pawlowsky

SWEET SUCCESS

12 Pou Dolç

Baixada de Sant Miquel, 6

Pou Dolç, opened in 1998 by young chefs Juan María Ribas and Sergio Mediavilla, quickly made a name for itself among the gourmands and design enthusiasts of Barcelona. Maria Caral and Xavier Puig helped turn the space over the 'sweet well' to industrial chic with their own elegant backdrop for Philippe Starck chairs and Ingo Maurer spotlights. Mediavilla now turns out the Mediterranean fusion cuisine that is 'a balanced diet, not a heavy meal but also not nouvelle cuisine'. In a dish of mini meatballs with tomatoes or sea bream and squid in meat broth with broad beans, the elements are meant to balance each other in 'absorption level' as well as flavour. Desserts range from a decadent chocolate torte with crème fraîche to a 'coulant', cool ice-cream with sponge and hot chocolate, to be eaten 'immediately' for best results. No problem there.

HAUTE BOHEMIAN

13 Slokai

Carrer del Palau, 5

Slokai is one of the more recent enterprises to take advantage of the upward trend of this area of new bohemia around the Escudellers. It's a restaurant and bar aimed at both the young crowd who parade these streets after dark and the more discriminating diner. It has an arthouse industrial interior by Christian Wincler, Ana Faseã and Gianfranco Vanella. Red panel screens, vivid paintings and pieces of designer furniture offset the ornate industrial steel columns. The food is a serious and somewhat experimental approach to fusion, 'a gastronomic journey', as they like to call it. There is a cold buffet at lunchtime but for dinner you can try *foie a la plancha con confitura de naranjas* (pâté platter with orange sauce) or *el magret de pato* (duck breast). Or opt for the house specialty: *la dorada con pisto y salsa de yema* (sea bream with mashed vegetables and a sort of hollandaise sauce). As the sign suggests, there is a strong Japanese element to some dishes, such as tuna marinated in soy sauce. Weekdays the background is soothing jazz by candlelight; weekends it's techno with visual projections.

BORN IN THE '50S

14 Again(st)

Carrer del Palau, 6

First you should know they open only in the afternoons, from 4:30 until 8:30, then that this is the source – with Gotham (see below) oddly close by – for design from the 1950s through the 1980s. Again(st) features French, Italian and Scandinavian pieces, as you would expect, but their most interesting stock is furniture and lighting by such Spanish designers as Sergio Mazza, Antoni Blanc and a number of unnamed artists, as well as plastics produced by the likes of Uldessa. Find bright bulbous leather sofas and chairs, space-age wall lights and saucer-style table lamps by Fase. It's a bright profusion of colour and design made more attractive by the friendly atmosphere.

RENEWED RETRO

15 Gotham

Carrer de Cervantes, 7

One of Barcelona's premier spots for mid-century modern design, Gotham is a favourite source for television and magazine stylists (*Wallpaper**), film directors (Pedro Almódovar) and collectors. Concentrating on furnishings and lighting from the 1930s, '50s, '60s and '70s, they carry mostly recent reproductions of classic designs. Among their most popular items, however, are pieces of inexpensive, functional Spanish cabinetry from the 1950s, which they restore and then spruce up with vibrant colours and patterns. Perhaps because they specialize in reproductions, there is a lighthearted and slightly whimsical air, a pleasant contrast to the often overly serious world of collecting.

GOTHAM

RESTAURANT
AGUT
FUNDAT 1924
VALENTINA
CROISSANT i
BEGUDA 2'00
ENTREPA i
BEGUDA 2'95
AMANIDES i
ENTREPANS PER
DINAR.

CLASSIC CATALAN

16 Agut

Carrer d'En Gignàs, 16

Along a narrow passageway, the warm wood interior set off by starched white tablecloths and upturned wineglasses lets you know you have come upon something special. The immaculate, old-world rooms are livened up with bold paintings – modern-style portraits, street scenes and bull fights – that recall something of the vivid tones of Impressionism but serve as an elegant backdrop for a very traditional menu. If you are looking for a classic Catalan meal that includes game as well as fish and seafood done to a high international standard, then this unpretentious address should be in your book.

CONSISTENTLY HIGH MARKS

17 Cafè de l'Academia

Carrer de Lledó, 1

This elegant little café/restaurant serves consistently good Catalan dishes at surprisingly reasonable prices and so is usually packed from the time it opens, even drawing a sizable crowd for breakfast, so to enjoy a really delightful lunch or dinner here it's advisable to book ahead. Being a stone's throw from the Generalitat means that a number of government officials are usually among the crowd, but that doesn't deter the friendly and very helpful staff from being just that. Whether you sit inside the quaint stone, wood-beamed dining room or, in good weather, at a table on the Plaça Sant Just, you'll enjoy starters of *torradeta de pernil* (cured ham on toasted bread) and *pintada rostida* (roast guinea fowl) and entrées of meat, game and fish. The fixed-price menu changes daily and usually includes a fresh fish or seafood option. For dessert, the chocolate *ganache* with orange is a necessary indulgence.

NEIGHBOURHOOD FAVOURITE

18 Bodega La Palma

Carrer de Palma de Sant Just, 7

This is your classic hole in the wall, an old-fashioned, family-run bar with a low-key, neighbourhood feel, quiet but welcoming. Huge wooden wine casks line one wall and the owner expertly taps them, as he has done for decades. A small, glowing place whose only real ornaments are the casks, the hanging ham and the 1950s paintings on the walls. It's almost hidden on a tiny side street off the quiet little Plaça de Sant Just. Great for a cosy pre-prandial drink, as it closes before 10pm most nights.

VIVA MEXICO

19 Valentina

Plaça del Regomir, 2

An inviting, modern café, art space and bookshop, Valentina opened only in 2002 but immediately began making its own contribution to brightening up the little Plaça del Regomir which it shares with a rather garish grocery store. This is a good spot to enjoy a quiet afternoon cup of tea and cake while looking over the regular art exhibitions and small but interesting display of books. Many of these focus on Mexican themes, as the café's name refers to a legendary female revolutionary leader. The art and books are laid out throughout the day (it opens after 4 pm), while documentaries are often screened in the evenings when the place fills up and Valentina becomes something more than the low-key curiosity on an otherwise blank square. From here it is an easy stroll to the clothes boutiques of Carrer d'Avinyó and the night-time attractions of Carrer dels Escudellers (see p. 33).

BARCE-LYON CHIC

20 Luka Home Made

Carrer de la Comtessa de Sobradiel, 10

Ludovic Charmot is a young Lyonnaise designer who opened this, his second outlet, in late 2002. The Luka-Home Made line, which he developed together with Karine Landon, favours unconventional cuts and shapes, some lacking traditional elements like sleeves or obvious necklines. Still, his use of interesting fabrics set off by angles and darts make the clothes not only tailored-looking but artfully so. And yet Charmot names 'comfort' as a primary objective. Home Made's profile has not skyrocketed just yet, but a certain London designer, who wouldn't be named, stopped in for a few inspirational items not long after the Barcelona shop opened.

1940S CLUB STYLE

21 Ginger

156

LACY DETAILS

22 Casa Oliveras

Carrer de Dagueria, 11

For four generations, since 1885, Casa Oliveras has produced handmade cotton lace trimmings, doilies, tablecloths and other accessories according to Spanish and Catalan tradition. The owner, Rosa Gallisa, who inherited the shop following on from her mother, grandmother and great-grandmother, is an expert in lace-making and offers classes in the back room for new enthusiasts. In addition to the rolls of traditionally made lace and other products, you can also buy patterns and all the materials needed for making your own, should you be feeling inspired. You can also get some invaluable advice.

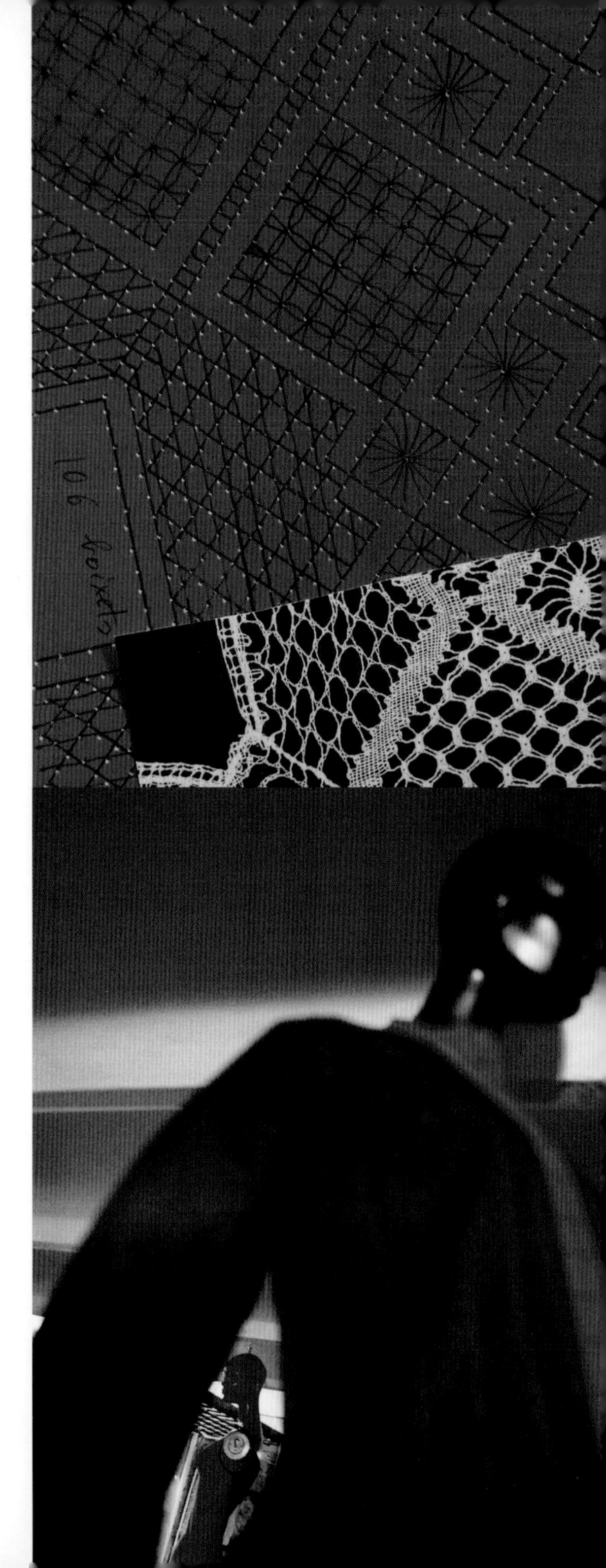

La Ribera
Barceloneta
Poble Nou

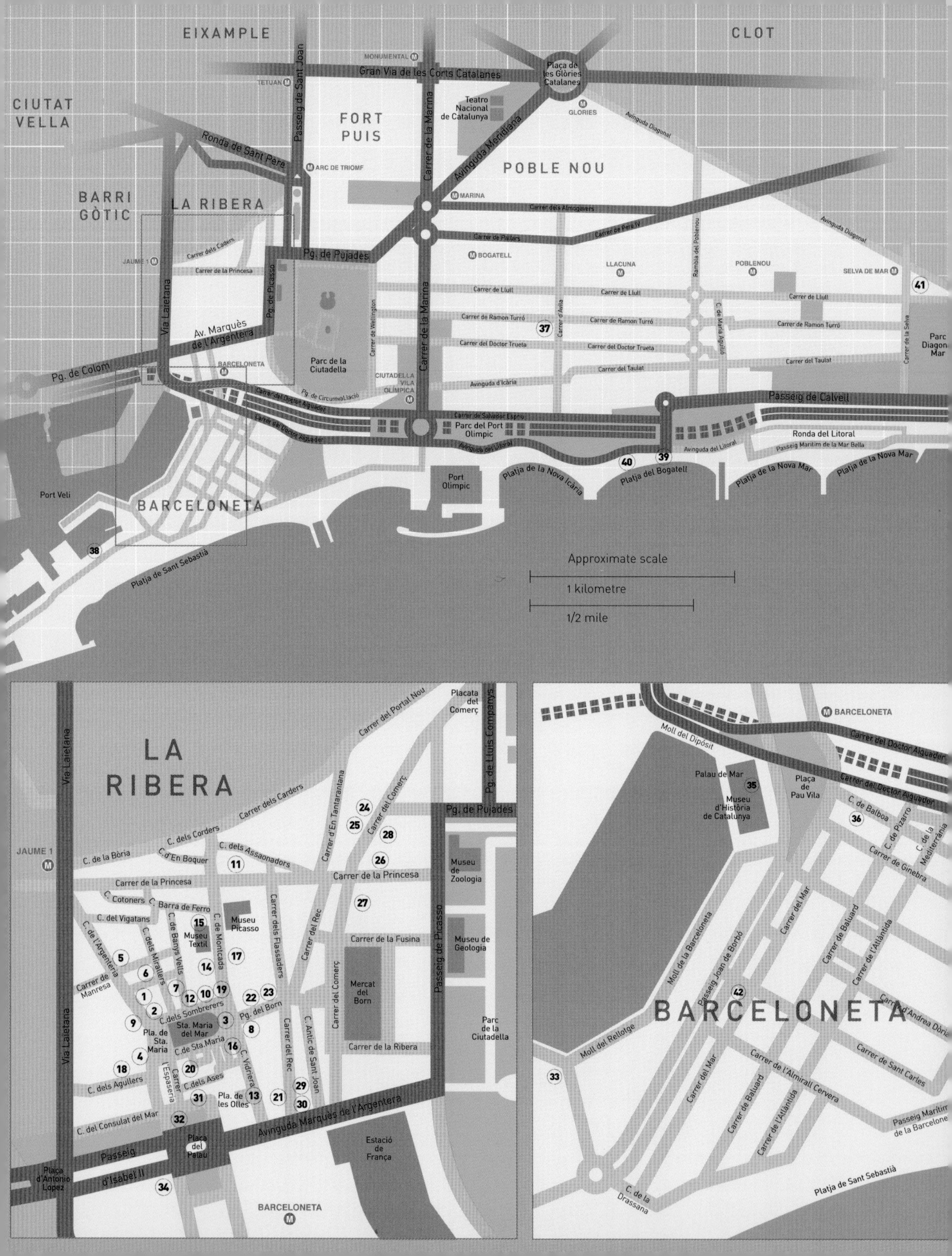
EIXAMPLE
CLOT
CIUTAT VELLA
FORT PUIS
POBLE NOU
BARRI GÒTIC
LA RIBERA
BARCELONETA
Gran Via de les Corts Catalanes
Plaça de les Glòries Catalanes
Teatro Nacional de Catalunya
Passeig de Sant Joan
Carrer de la Marina
Avinguda Meridiana
Avinguda Diagonal
Ronda de Sant Pere
Pg. de Pujades
Via Laietana
Pg. de Picasso
Av. Marquès de l'Argentera
Pg. de Colom
Parc de la Ciutadella
Passeig de Calvell
Parc del Port Olimpic
Ronda del Litoral
Port Olimpic
Port Vell
Platja de la Nova Icària
Platja del Bogatell
Platja de la Nova Mar
Platja de Sant Sebastià
Approximate scale
1 kilometre
1/2 mile
Carrer de la Princesa
Mercat del Born
Museu Picasso
Museu Textil
Sta. Maria del Mar
Museu de Zoologia
Museu de Geologia
Estació de França
Plaça del Palau
Passeig d'Isabel II
Palau de Mar
Museu d'Història de Catalunya
Plaça de Pau Vila
Moll del Dipòsit
Moll de la Barceloneta
Passeig Joan de Borbó
Moll del Rellotge
Carrer del Doctor Aiguader
Carrer de l'Almirall Cervera
Passeig Marítim de la Barceloneta

In the Ribera is the city's most famed medieval street, the Carrer de Montcada, whose vaulted palatial residences were first built in the 14th century for the city burghers and merchants. For centuries, until the development of the Eixample, these were the most prestigious addresses in Barcelona. All are well preserved, many now housing public galleries such as the Museu Picasso and Museu Tèxtil i d'Indumentària (p. 50), others home to quirky shops and the city's one bar devoted to the Baroque (see p. 50). Over the past decades, the ground-floor spaces have filled up with artisans keen to take advantage of what used to be cheap rates for their *tallers* (studios) and shops, and despite the recent sharp rise of property prices, craftspeople still base themselves in the Ribera. In a city known historically for its textiles and crafts, they offer everything from hand-woven textiles to silver, ceramics, glass and other applied arts.

In the last few years, one of the most quickly gentrifying and most talked-about areas of Barcelona has been that around the Passeig del Born, once a jousting ground, later the place where a young Antoni Gaudí lived (at Placeta de Montcada, 12) when he first came to Barcelona to study architecture. Until the last ten years, however, it was an overlooked part of the old city. Today it is a leafy pedestrianized square, lined with lively bars and clubs, which attract insomniac revellers. Many restaurants, cafés and boutiques followed, but the result is not overly commercialized, not yet anyway. More recently the compact area has seen the arrival of the city's brightest and most adventurous restaurants, many run by chefs who represent the new wave of Catalan cuisine.

Barceloneta, which links the Ribera with the shoreline, was laid out in a grid plan in the 18th century after Philip V made one of many attempts to seize control of the unwieldy Catalans. Today it retains the aura of the fishing village, with the houses in an ordered, if tight, progression, with a number the ground-floor spaces given over to restaurants and bars where seafood is usually the house speciality. It's not difficult to avoid the overtouristed establishments along the shore and piers brought on by the harbourside regeneration by simply going inland.

Northwest of Barceloneta, the outlying neighbourhood of Poble Nou (new town) is less polished than its name suggests, but here in a somewhat commercially neglected area below the bottom portion of the Diagonal, properties are slowly starting to be taken up by artists forced out the Barri Gòtic and adventurous entrepreneurs, such as the clubbing impresarios at Oven (p. 57). Some might prefer locales like Rancho Grande (p. 137), untouched by urban redevelopment and benefiting only from the cyclical nature resonant in a city preoccupied with the project of self-betterment.

GRAND OLD GASTRONOMY

1 Senyor Parellada

Carrer de l'Argenteria, 37

Ramón Parellada's recent investment in the Hotel Banys Orientals (p. 120), which is above, as well as his interest in La Vinya del Senyor (p. 151), a few blocks down, makes him something of a local legend. But it is the restaurant, opened in 1955 and used by the hotel for breakfast service, that made his name and his reputation. A distinctly formal affair, with velvet-wrapped crystal chandeliers and white-aproned waiters, potted palms and piano music, the whole thing has a sort of Jazz Age expectancy about it. But the food is purely traditional Catalan and proud of it, though the mode of presentation (more tasting menu/tapas-style) has been modernized in recent years: grilled shrimp, *baccalà* (salt cod), *lloganissa* (sausage) *de Caldes, sípia a la planxa* (grilled cuttlefish), *sopa de peix* (fish soup). The atmosphere is friendlier than the crisp formality suggests and staff are very helpful with the menu.

FASHIONABLE NEW FAVOURITE

2 Hotel Banys Oriental

120

SOARING GOTHIC

3 Esglèsia Santa Maria del Mar

Plaça de Santa Maria/Passeig del Born

'There is no grander or more solemn architectural space in Spain than Santa Maria del Mar', says art critic Robert Hughes, and indeed, despite its absence of ornament, of a multitude of spires and fretwork, it bespeaks grandeur as if the vaulted space has opened up to the world beyond. It's a fortunate oddity of church architecture that it can amplify space even while enclosing it. Completed in 1383 (in just over 60 years), Santa Maria del Mar, with its hulking columns supporting ribbon-like ribbed vaulting, the contrast of heavy stone and increasingly delicate structure creating the illusion of infinite height, is a prime example of Catalan Gothic. The fact that its Baroque decoration was largely destroyed during the Civil War little diminishes the impact of its soaring interior, lit by delicate stained-glass windows, or the sense of awe.

WINE AND SNACKS

4 La Vinya del Senyor

151

WONDERFULLY WOVEN

5 Estudi Tèxtil del Born

Carrer del Brosolí, 1 local 4

Anna Vilafranca's small atelier and shop is about as full of character and artisanal authenticity as the centuries-old building that she inhabits. Here she works at her loom creating the fabric for beautifully woven scarves, shawls, jackets and skirts on display against the rugged stone walls, which make a nicely contrasting backdrop for the soft, hand-finished articles. Wool, cotton and silk feature in winter; in summer she uses more linen and ramie. She also weaves jute rugs, and much of the fabric is hand-dyed. In a city known for its textiles, Vilafranca is one its most inspired creators.

TACTILE BEAUTY

6 Mar Rodriguez

170

WELL-AGED WINE BAR

7 Va de Vi

Carrer de Banys Vells, 16

The centuries-old stone caverns of the ground floors of these buildings make particularly atmospheric wine bars and local artist Josep Maria Cases has made the most of these 16th-century assets, adding some modern touches, like a glass bar and a few design-conscious lighting features that come together to form a homey but subtly stylish drinking venue. There is a lot of space to sit or stand beneath the stone arches and sample some of the many wines that Cases feels so passionately about and which inspired him to begin this venture a few years ago. Among the reds by the glass, the Traslanzas Tempranillo de Cigalés is one of the more memorable. Wine isn't the only thing Cases feels strongly about: he also sells snacks featuring 'artisanal' produce such as Iberian, acorn-fed pork, ham, salami and sausages, Catalan and other Spanish cheeses and smoked and cured fish.

HAND-PAINTED ACCESSORIES

8 Atalanta Manufactura

Passeig del Born, 10

Here, in the hub of craft-conscious Barcelona, art and fashion come together in bold harmony. Beautiful, hand-painted designs for silk scarves, handkerchiefs, waistcoats and fabrics are created in the workshop while a boutique sells them directly to the eager public. A window into the workshop means you can actually see the artists at their painstaking task. In the shop some of the art-historical references (paintings, sculpture) used to inspire motifs or a fanciful play on art are displayed alongside the finished pieces.

GOURMET LESSONS

9 Hofmann

135

FUTURISTIC FABRICS

10 Konrad Muhr

Carrer dels Sombrerers, 25

Around the corner from the historic Carrer de Montcada (p. 50), designer Toni Morral, also known as Konrad Muhr, whole-heartedly embraces the future with his cool, urban approach to men's and women's clothing turned out in the latest fabrics, such as Kevlar, neoprene and variations on plastics, as well as leather and fish net. There are some natural fabrics too, but most pieces have a crisp, uniformed look, despite being flamboyantly avant-garde. Some items in this, the Barcelona designer's only shop, are one-offs, signed and numbered by Morral, who has dressed Spanish celebrities and writes regularly on fashion and culture.

ENATE
ENATE
ENATE

THE DESIGNERS' OUTLET

11 On Land

171

ROASTED DELIGHTS

12 E & A Gispert

174

ART OF THE T-SHIRT

13 Custo

166

CASUAL CAVA AND TAPAS

14 El Xampanyet

Carrer de Montcada, 22

As the name suggests, this is a place known for its Cava, but just as sparkling wine in Spain does not promote the same degree of pretension as it does in various other countries, neither do the bars, generally, that sell the stuff. The colourful tiles, stacked casks hung with a variety of novelty bottle-openers, well-worn interior and typical selection of counter-kept tapas (including anchovies – *anxoves* – with a famously secret sauce) bespeak the informal, comfortable atmosphere for which this family-run operation is well-known and well-loved. The drinks themselves are just about the best antidotes to anything, including the crowds meandering the Carrer de Montcada.

FRESH AND FRIENDLY

15 Tèxtil Café

Carrer de Montcada, 12

The little café in the restored courtyard of the Palau dels Marquesos de Llió, home to the Museu Tèxtil, is a modern little place serving coffee and tea and sandwiches as well as café-menu meals and wine for lunch and dinner. The stone vaults of the ground floor and cobbled courtyard are offset with glass and works of art. The place manages to catch the energetic atmosphere of the popular area for visitors without being the least bit bland or common.

MASTER OF ACCESSORIES

16 Rafa Teja Atelier

162

ANTIQUE PLEASURES

17 Carrer de Montcada

- Galeria Maeght, no. 25
- Espai Baroque, no. 20
- Papers Coma, no. 20
- Museu Picasso, no. 15
- Museu Tèxtil i d'Indumentària, 12–14

It's almost impossible to miss either this narrow historical street or its stream of tourists flowing in, out and around the Museu Picasso, but it's a walk worth taking, especially if you remember to note a few imperatives. This is one of the best-preserved medieval streets in Barcelona possibly because until the creation of the Eixample in the 19th century, this was the city's premier address. The three-storey houses with their wide gated entrances and spacious interior courtyards were built for the town grandees; those surviving are mostly 15th-century and have now been taken over by an array of cultural organizations as well as a few nice bars. At no. 25 is the Barcelona branch of the high-end Galeria Maeght, which features mainly 20th-century modern masters. The Palau Dalmases, at no. 20, is one of the grandest residences and home to the Omnium Cultural, as well as the bar-performance venue Espai Baroque, which creates a rather bizarre Baroque atmosphere of art, furnishings and musical programmes. The velvet draperies beckon enticingly to those peering in from the street. Papers Coma is easily overlooked in the throng of galleries and boutiques along this historic street, but the range of papers, laid, woven, tinted and pressed with bits of coloured fibre, is worth a look as the colours and mixtures are not your usual range. It also carries crafted gift bags, notebooks and wraps.

The ineluctably popular Museu Picasso, housed in the wonderful Palau Berenguer d'Aguilar, attracts large crowds, but the collection leaves some wishing for more. The grand Palau, with its five bays and well-kept arcade was restored by Enric Sòria and Jordi Garcés and enhances the experience. No. 12 marks the worthwhile destination of the Museu Tèxtil i d'Indumentària, where cloth and costumes are on display, commemorating the city's historic association with textile production. The appealing café (see previous page) and sophisticated craft-centred boutique have been gracefully inserted into the courtyard.

OENOPHILE'S DELIGHT

18 Vila Viniteca

173

SAND

APPLIED ARTS

19 Montcada • Taller

Placeta de Montcada, 10 bis

At the corner of Carrer de Montcada and Sombrerers, the Montcada Taller, like the Estudi Tèxtil (p. 46), sums up the creative atmosphere of this area of Barcelona. If you are drawn to textiles and knitwear, handmade jewelry, ceramics and glassware, then the Montcada Taller should be on your day's itinerary, along with the Museu Picasso, as it showcases local designers living in Barcelona, most of them Spanish and many of them young people studying their craft in one of the nearby design schools.

DARK, WARM, WELCOME

20 La Morera

Carrer del Fossar de les Moreres, 5

On the spartan Fossar de les Moreres (modernized in 1989) a towering sculptural metal arc was erected to commemorate the spot where soldiers defending Barcelona from the Bourbon incursion in 1714 were buried (in the cemetery of the *moreres*, 'mulberry trees'). Otherwise, the square itself is rather disappointing except for the border of interesting shops and bars. Of these, La Morera offers cocktails and wine in a close, atmospheric setting achieved with lots of candles and red draperies against stone walls. The bar continues downstairs in an even more ambient cellar room.

WORTH ITS SALT

21 Salero

Carrer del Rec, 60

The white-on-white décor, bestowed by designer Pilar Libano (see Lydia Delgado, p. 169, and Antonio Miro, p. 168), is not the only thing that distinguishes it from the more colourful Abac across the way. Despite its obvious high marks for style, Salero is not in the same league in terms of pricing and high cuisine. But its popularity with fashion and media people and a large collection of well-informed fans is very high indeed. So too is its success in somewhat pioneering fusion cuisine that includes Japanese elements like seaweed and a kangaroo entrée, as well as more standard Catalan fish and seafood. The wine list focuses on select Spanish varieties. Open for breakfast and afternoon tea, as well as for dinner, Salero has become a favourite for modern, alternative dining.

BIRTH OF THE COOL

22 Passeig del Born

- Sandwich & Friends, no. 27
- La Cocotte, no. 16

Starting east and working your way west along this former jousting ground that is now a tree-lined pedestrianized zone, you'll first encounter the large, barnlike structure that resembles a Victorian covered market done in corrugated metal with some nice decorative elements designed by Josep Fontserè (see the Mercat de Sant Antoni, p. 74). This is all undergoing work as part of the recent, fast-paced gentrification of El Born. Sandwich & Friends, near the corner of Carrer del Rec, is one of the modern, bright, friendly establishments that have popped up in recent years. The bold yellow interior and cartoon mural by Jordi Labanda will get your attention, as will the 50 or so different rolled sandwiches, all named after friends of the owners. Come for a coffee or a snack, especially during the day when the bars all have their shutters down. Still heading towards the Santa Maria del Mar you'll encounter attractions left and right (literally). From old favourites like the Pitín Bar (see p. 152) and Miramelindo (no.15) which is Cuban-inspired and was popular before the El Born renaissance to the futuristic frolics at the Plastic Bar (see p. 152). But if it's too early for drinking you can also try the New York–diner style of La Cocotte for eating in or take away. They pride themselves on international cooking but it's the style, the location and the vibrant mood that make this place a hit.

PARTY CENTRAL

23 Passeig del Born

152

INDUSTRIAL FUSION

24 Comerç 24

CHOCOLATE-COATED HISTORY

25 Museu de la Xocolata

Plaça de Pons i Clerch

In a city bewitched by the stuff, many are at pains to demonstrate the beneficial properties of chocolate, among them the ICC (Instituto del Cacao y el Chocolate) and the Gremi Provincial de Pastisseria de Barcelona (the Pastry-makers' Guild), which has opened this fascinating museum attached to its cooking school. The Museu, set in a small modernized space next to the chocolate factory rooms, offers a short course on the history, the manufacture, the cuisine and the world popularity of the humble cacao plant. Learn about Hernán Cortés's introduction of chocolate to Europe in 1519 with the exotic 'xocolatl' drink, as well as the many medicinal uses (for example, as an aphrodisiac). There is also a small but enchanting gift stall selling chocolate in many shapes and sizes as well as T-shirts and chocolate-based literature. You can treat yourself to a hot cup at the bar.

SWEET SURRENDER

26 Espai Sucre

THE WILD SIDE

27 Bestiari

Carrer del Comerç, 25

The primary-coloured wall mural that dominates the interior is a sort of Keith Haring–meets–Picasso, but is the work of Carlos Vaonza, a member of the Madrid-based group Beozar who chose Barcelona as the location to unite their artistic collective with a culinary enterprise. Opened in 2002, Bestiari is well placed in a neighbourhood that has become the heart of the city for the hip and arty crowd. Chef Javier Garcia produces Mediterranean fusion cuisine that is a different kind of art. In addition to the permanent works on the walls, temporary exhibitions of contemporary art are also held.

BRIGHT YOUNG STAR

28 Santa Maria

MODERN CLASSIC

29 Abac

REBIRTH OF THE COOL

30 Park Hotel

STAR-QUALITY TAPAS

31 La Estrella de Plata

THE CHEF KNOWS BEST

32 Passadis del Pep

PORTSIDE DINING

33 Restaurant Barceloneta

L'Escar, 22, Moll dels Pescadors

Named for the port area, which it overlooks, Barceloneta is a large, spacious restaurant sited in a nondescript building at the end of the quay. There are two levels upstairs (one is for private parties), with terrace dining and a wide range of fish and seafood, as well as meat dishes on offer. In fact, with the rustic maritime décor it all looks a little more commercialized than it actually is. The fish and seafood are as fresh as the morning's catch and well-prepared according to traditional recipes (*a la plancha, a la romana, bacallà* – grilled platter, fried in batter or traditional salt cod). But the *fumet*, smoked fish, is also worth a try. The recommended wine list offers some interesting Spanish varieties. And the view over the harbour just adds to the flavour.

N SO
1903

PORTES

DOORS OF DISTINCTION

34 Restaurant 7 Portes

Passeig d'Isabel II, 14

It has been sitting under the colonnade of the Plaça del Palau since 1836, being the oldest restaurant in the city, but has lost little of its appeal in all those years. The lattice-paned windows and white curtains frame a scene of classic Catalan dining amid palms and mirrors. Formally attired waiters whisk around serving up traditional rice-based and seafood dishes, with house specialties that include *paella de Parellada*, the *gran plato de mariscos* (seafood platter) and *botifarra* (Catalan sausage). There are also pasta dishes and other concessions to the numerous tourists, all produced by head chef Josep Lladonosa, who has a reputation almost as well established as these premises. However, if you stick to the Catalan classics you'll experience the best quality.

HARBOUR-SIDE DRINKS

35 La Miranda del Museu

151

CLASSIC CERVECERIA

36 El Vaso de Oro

159

HOT AND SPICY

37 Oven

Carrer de Ramon Turró, 126

The red-heated glow of the interior or the sizzling popularity here would warm you, whatever the temperature or the crowd. Oven is a wide-open space of a restaurant, bar, 'chill-out' zone, exhibition area and garden, so the oozing reds help to focus and create some intimacy for dining within the art-warehouse framework. Beyond the glow there is a lot going on design-wise, which justifies the trip out to Poble Nou even if the food were not also exceptional. It's also a great place to go for a late-night drink (open until 3:30 am Thursday through Sunday evenings) and for live and DJ-mastered music by Barcelona funksters De Lippo and Professor Angel Dust, who have a special interest in the place. Catch them at La Paloma (see p. 73) when they're not in residence here.

CUISINE ON HIGH

38 Torre d'Alta Mar

143

SAND AND SERENITY

39 Platja del Bogatell

Passeig Marítim del Bogatell

Since the Olympic regeneration schemes of the late 1980s and early 1990s, Barcelona's beaches have been given a new lease of life and are now popular with natives and tourists alike. Wide and sandy, with lots of refreshment nearby, they offer an enticing afternoon of relaxation. The Platja del Bogatell, being slightly removed from the main access areas, offers a little more quiet.

SEAFOOD AND CAKES

40 Xiringuito Escribà

Litoral Mar, 42 (Platja del Bogatell)

The beachfront used to be full of ramshackle little *xiringuitas* (open-air restaurants) before redevlopment swept them away. This is one of the best remaining, a distinctly upmarket version, glass-walled for unimpeded views, and owned by the same pastry-making family as Escribà (p. 149). They do have lots of desserts on the menu but you'll want to get into the seafood first. The chefs work away on small tabletop burners so that pans sizzle with *fideuà* or *paella* chock-full of prawns and shellfish in clear view. There are also tapas platters to share, *bacallà, arroz negro de tinta de sepia* and other traditional seafood dishes. They warn that the *paella* will take twenty minutes, which is even more painful since you get to watch (and smell) it all bubbling to perfection.

HOME ON THE RANGE

41 El Rancho Grande

137

OLD-FASHIONED FINERY

42 Can Solé

Carrer de Sant Carles, 4

The front of the building tells you that it's been here since 1903. A quick look around says that it's been well loved and equally well preserved during that time. There are lots of vintage photographs of Barcelona on the walls and the tiles outside show the harvesting of seafood and produce, the staples of the menu. The atmosphere is formal but friendly, being far enough off the tourist route to maintain a good number of well-dressed local clientele who come again and again for the wonderfully fresh seafood in paella, grilled platters and soups. There are a host of special dishes featuring lobster, prawns, octopus and whatever is fresh for the season. Ask for the recommendations.

03

El Raval
Montjuïc

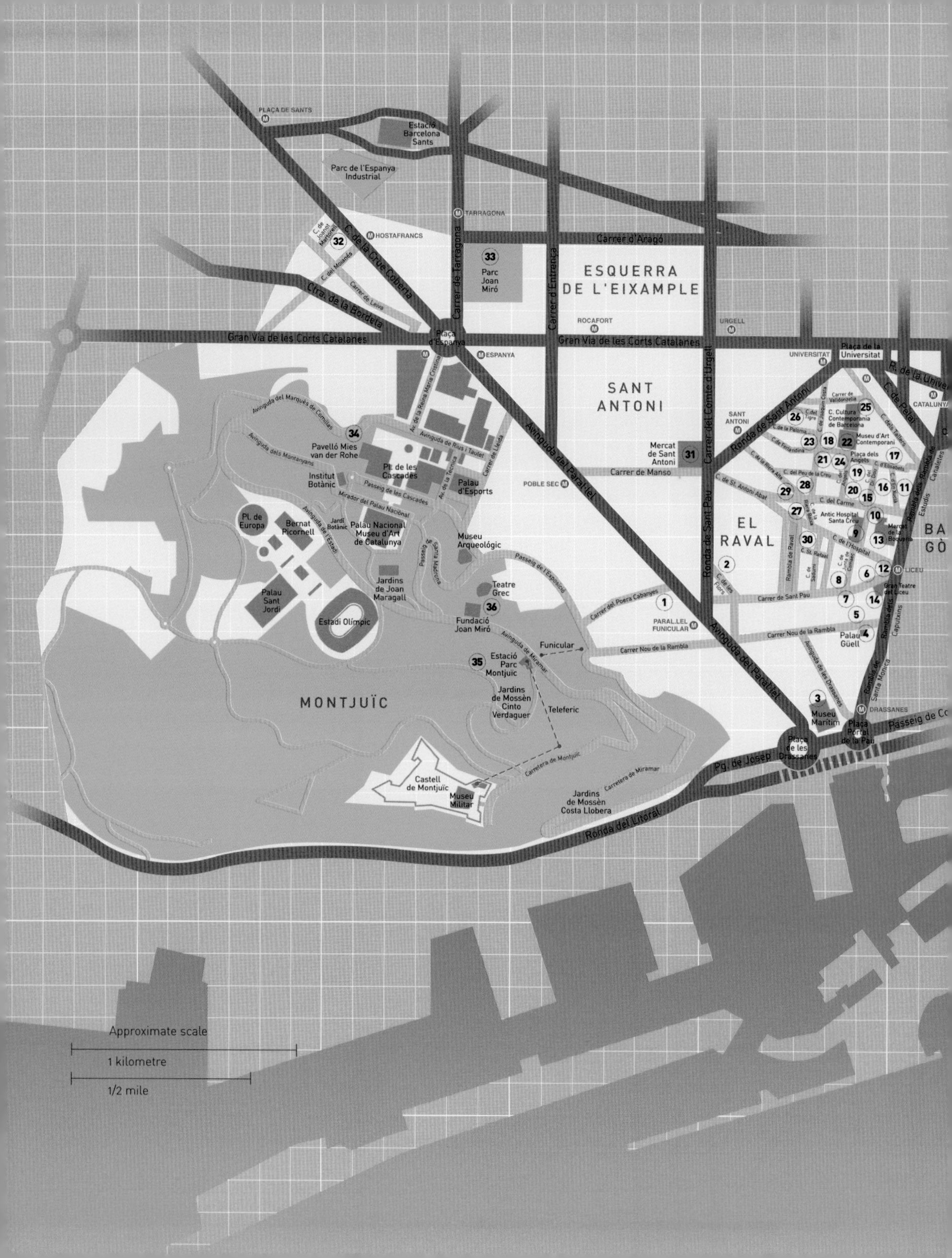

PLAÇA DE SANTS
Estació Barcelona Sants
Parc de l'Espanya Industrial
TARRAGONA
HOSTAFRANCS
Carrer d'Aragó
ESQUERRA DE L'EIXAMPLE
Parc Joan Miró
Carrer de Tarragona
Carrer d'Entença
C. de la Creu Coberta
Ctra. de la Bordeta
ROCAFORT
URGELL
Gran Via de les Corts Catalanes
Plaça d'Espanya
ESPANYA
UNIVERSITAT
Plaça de la Universitat
CATALUNYA
SANT ANTONI
Ronda de Sant Antoni
Carrer del Comte d'Urgell
Mercat de Sant Antoni
Carrer de Manso
POBLE SEC
Avinguda del Paral·lel
Avinguda del Marquès de Comillas
Avinguda dels Montanyans
Pavelló Mies van der Rohe
Pl. de les Cascades
Institut Botànic
Passeig de les Cascades
Mirador del Palau Nacional
Palau d'Esports
Pl. de Europa
Bernat Picornell
Jardí Botànic
Palau Nacional Museu d'Art de Catalunya
Museu Arqueològic
Passeig de l'Exposició
Jardins de Joan Maragall
Teatre Grec
Palau Sant Jordi
Estadi Olímpic
Fundació Joan Miró
Funicular
Estació Parc Montjuïc
MONTJUÏC
Jardins de Mossèn Cinto Verdaguer
Teleferic
Castell de Montjuïc
Museu Militar
Carretera de Montjuïc
Carretera de Miramar
Jardins de Mossèn Costa Llobera
Ronda del Litoral
EL RAVAL
Ronda de Sant Pau
PARAL.LEL FUNICULAR
Carrer del Poeta Cabanyes
Carrer de Sant Pau
Carrer Nou de la Rambla
Palau Güell
Museu Marítim
Plaça de les Drassanes
Plaça Portal de la Pau
DRASSANES
Passeig de Colom
Pg. de Josep
C. Cultura Contemporània de Barcelona
Museu d'Art Contemporani
Plaça dels Àngels
Antic Hospital Santa Creu
Mercat de la Boqueria
LICEU
Gran Teatre del Liceu
Rambla del Raval
Rambla de Santa Mònica
Caputxins
Canaletes
Estudis
C. de Pelai
Approximate scale
1 kilometre
1/2 mile

Although the street demarcating the medieval quarter was for centuries considered outside of Barcelona proper, in recent years it, like much of Barcelona, has experienced a revival of fortune as one of Europe's most famous pedestrian passages, the Ramblas. The mile-long, tree-lined meridien promenade that we see today was planted and laid out in the 18th-century and encompasses five streets following on from one another. It was a favourite of writers and artists until, like many parts of Barcelona, it fell into woeful neglect before being rescued during Olympic regeneration. Having become a first stop for all visitors (and the accompanying street performers and pickpockets), the Ramblas might not be to everyone's taste, but as an urban focal point its appeal is undeniable. In its heyday the Ramblas was a showplace of the wealth gained through industry, signs of which can be seen in Modernista shopfronts like that at Escribà (p. 149), in the regal façade of Gaudí's Palau Güell (p. 63) and in the reconstruction of the 19th-century Gran Teatre del Liceu (p. 67).

The Raval, to the west of the Ramblas, was known for its monastery buildings, which were pulled down or reinhabited in the 19th-century, and the bountiful produce market La Boqueria (see p. 67) was given a permanent address on the site of a ruined convent. But while in Picasso's time it was an area known for its vices, drinking, prostitution and vagrancy, today it has been touched by the golden wand of regeneration, though it remains a neighbourhood of wide ethnic diversity, youthful energy and creativity. New design is tapping into that creative spirit that such culture brings, catalyzed perhaps by the arrival of the Richard Meier–designed Museu d'Art Contemporani de Barcelona (MACBA, p. 71) and its sister project, the Centre de Cultura Contemporània de Barcelona (CCCB), sited in the adjoining 1802 Casa de la Caritat. Gradually, the Plaça and Carrer dels Àngels have filled with galleries and arty bar-restaurants, and some of the city's most eye-opening new interiors are located around Carrer del Carme, a street otherwise untouched. There are still plenty of classic old drinking, dancing and eating spots, enlivened by students from the nearby university, leaving something of the old edgy appeal intact.

Southwest and reached by a short ride on the funicular you cross the modern residential overspill to the summit of Montjuïc, the 'mountain of Jove', or 'of the Jews', depending on which legend takes your fancy. A mostly dry and uninhabited projection, it became an ideal site for the Olympic Stadium and its consequent structures. Now with Mies van der Rohe's reconstructed seminal modern pavilion, the Fundació Joan Miró and the Museu Nacional d'Art Catalunya, all surrounded by landscaped botanical gardens, Montjuïc has become its own cultural capital on a hill.

2'60
19'25
11,45
13'20
24'00
RIOJA
Rioja Bordón
13'50
11'70
19'25
12'00
28'00
15'00
10'50
27'65
18'00
BOWMORE
Malt Scotch Whisky
1971
GLENMORANGIE
SINGLE HIGHLAND
SHERRY WOOD FINISH
MADEIRA WOOD FINISH
PORT WOOD FINISH
Vins a Copes
29.00
156'30
37.30
JOAN D'ANGUERA
PINORD
Chateldon
CABERNET SAUVIGNON
MONTE NERY
1996
Faustino I
3'00
1'80
1'10
1'80
1'50
2'50

CATALAN SUSHI

1 Quimet i Quimet

Carrer del Poeta Cabanyas, 25

A tapas bar that has been through the generations, Quimet is now run by the son and daughter of the owners who have to struggle a bit to keep up with the numbers who crowd in to eat standing up, often without even gaining purchase on counter space. They specialize in cold platters of smoked or cured meats and fish like salmon and yoghurt or tomato, mussel and caviar *tostadas* as well as various types of marinated fish, beans, olives and chilies, a lot of which can be purchased in tins behind the counter. Wash it all down with a cool glass of Cava, which will probably have to be passed over to you by the very friendly regular clientele.

CUISINE OF KINGS

2 Ca l'Isidre

ANCIENT MARINERS

3 Museu Maritim

Avinguda de les Drassanes

In the old port (Port Vell) stands one of the most intriguing examples of secular Gothic architecture in Europe. The Drassanes Reials (Royal Shipyards) of Barcelona were originally built between 1283 and 1390 and were used for shipbuilding for the Catalan–Aragonese Navy until the 17th century. The complex of Gothic naves set on stone pillars with a gable roof is the best-preserved of any such buildings in the Mediterranean. Since 1937 the shipyards have housed Barcelona's Maritime Museum, chronicling the city's inextricable relationship with the sea. Very recent improvements by architects Esteve and Robert Terradas i Muntañola (who also designed the new seafront aquarium) and modernized exhibition spaces have made it a truly unique marriage of education and cultural heritage. One of the star exhibits is an exact replica of the Royal Galley of Juan of Austria, built to celebrate the 400th anniversary of the Battle of Lepanto. An unexpected bonus is the appealing café-restaurant that is far above your average museum-dining experience.

EMERGING GAUDÍ

4 Palau Güell

Carrer Nou de la Rambla, 3–5

In 1885, after Gaudí had finished a gatehouse and outbuildings for the Pedralbes estate of his friend, industrial tycoon Don Eusebi Güell, Güell commissioned him to build a new house. It was to be in the unlikely location of the Raval, which at the time was known more for prostitution and debauchery than for its bourgeois palaces. Güell was also a great patron of the arts and as the Universal Exposition of 1888 was approaching, the house would be expected to make a significant statement with regard to Catalan culture. Gaudí was up to the task and produced this fascinating interplay between order and whimsicality. The symmetrical arches on the ground floor, sharp geometric forms and placement of the main reception rooms on the first floor all appear to adhere to strict rules of form. But then there are rebellious asymmetries, ornate ironwork and, as in other buildings like the Casa Milà, rooftop ventilation shafts cast in fanciful organic shapes, with no two alike. The interior contains all the spaces needed for a member of the social and business elite – office space and grand salons for entertaining surrounding a central hall – but with Gaudí's peculiar blend of Gothic, Mudéjar and Baroque elements mixing in a barely restrained fantasy (see also Casa Vicens, p. 103, Casa Batlló, p. 86, and Casa Milà/La Pedrera, p. 93).

CLUB TROPICANA

5 Salsitas

DRINK IN THE ATMOSPHERE

6 Hotel España

AGELESS APPEAL

7 **Marsella**

Carrer de Sant Pau, 65

It shows its age in the dusty, ancient bottles locked away in an old wooden cabinet, in the crystal chandeliers which have lost a bit of their sparkle and in the patchwork of tiles on the floor. But this bar, run by generations of the same family, wears it well, with an enthusiastic clientele that keeps the rooms humming, the glasses clanking merrily and the tables usually full until closing time. A convenient and suitably contrasting spot for a post-prandial drink after dinner at Biblioteca (see below).

READ–EAT–DRINK

8 **Biblioteca**

Carrer de Junta de Comerç, 28

Head chef Iñake Lopez worked in a number of restaurants abroad, including the legendary Rules in London, before heading back to Barcelona with his Irish partner, Mary Finn, in 2001 to open Biblioteca, a restaurant, Mary says, 'based on the principle of fresh food that retains as much of its original flavour and texture as possible'. Eschewing precious architecture and complicated presentations for a large, open kitchen serving up the freshest possible fish, seafood and market produce from the nearby Boqueria, Lopez and Finn have attracted the attention of other professionals who come to watch the chef in action and to purchase some of the cookery books in Spanish, French and English that are not widely available in the city. The Mediterranean menu (with Basque and Irish influences) features marinated tuna, *suquet* (stew) of clams, cockles and scorpion fish or wild mushroom *paella* among its seasonal specialties. The pastries (for example, a wafer-thin apple tart) and bread are home-made daily.

HOLY EXPO

9 **Sala Exposicions La Capella**

Carrer de l'Hospital, 56

Around the corner from the clamorous Boqueria market the disused chapel of Hospital Santa Creu has been turned into an evocative little meditative space for art. It's actually two spaces: the Sala Gran and the Sala Petita. Both retain the unornamented stone interiors linking it with the 15th-century hospital, which was the main medical facility of Barcelona until 1930, when Domènech i Montaner's glorious Modernista design for the Hospital de la Santa Creu i Sant Pau was completed. The gothic Hospital, where Gaudí died after being hit by a trolley car, is now

25.20
St JOSEP
LA BOQUERIA
BAR PINOTXO
4'50
2'50
2'50
2'90
Pimientos
0,99
03
Rovellons
4'99

home to the Biblioteca de Catalunya. The ward buildings, which give entrance to the library from Carrer del Carme, and Gothic cloisters (1415–17) now enclose a large garden space. The Capella brings the medieval buildings alive to the moment, with shows by young local artists and by hosting international collaborative projects.

STUNNING NEW FAVOURITE

10 Lupino

Carrer del Carme, 33

A fantastically sleek, modern intervention by German designer Ellen Rapeulius makes a subtle but noticeable presence on this largely ungentrified street. Lupino has all the streamlined, gleaming promise of the best new restaurant-lounges and a little more. Come just for the beautiful design and bar scene, which are special enough. Stroll down the glamorous backlit green walkway and settle in and try some of the Barcelona fusion cuisine by Catalan chef Txiqui Fuster, which includes starters of *milhojas de patata y confit de pato* (sliced potatoes with duck confit); *'cassoulette' de setas* (mushrooms); *tempura de verduritas* (vegetables) or *crema Japonesa d'espinaca* (Japanese-style creamed spinach). Main courses include biriyani dishes and traditional meat and fish, such as Iberian beef with smoked apples. The bar scene is upmarket and the cocktail craze thriving.

WITH CREAM ON TOP

11 Granja M. Viader

Carrer d'En Xuclà, 4–6

Started in 1870, the Granja ('farm' or 'dairy') Viader is what the Catalans refer to as a 'milk bar'. It also has a deli attached selling a selection of cured meats and local cheeses. But that is not the reason to go. What draws the afternoon crowd – admittedly many ladies of a certain age – is the wonderfully decadent chocolate 'Suizo', a cup of pudding-thick hot chocolate topped with a sizeable lump of unsweetened fresh cream. Hold on to your waistline and preferably a spoon. And if you think that's naughty, just have a look around you at the folks who order theirs with small biscuits or, even better, sugar-dusted pastries.

CAKES AND ART

12 Escribà

149

MARKET FRESH

13 Mercat de la Boqueria Sant Josep

- La Maseria de la Boqueria
- Pinotxo

There has been a market here for centuries. As the city grew and boundaries changed, the market stayed roughly where it had always been but a scheme was enacted to create a structure on the grounds of the old convent of the Carmelites of Sant Josep. So the ramshackle collection of stalls was organized in a porticoed square (1836–40), which was never completely finished but covered over with the metal structure in 1860. Today it is still the best place to buy fresh produce in Barcelona. It's crowded and noisy but clean, well-organized and bountiful with rows of individual stalls filled with all manner of goods. Though you may not need many provisions for a short stay in the city, have a stroll through La Boqueria anyway and choose some exceptional treats for a Catalan gourmet picnic or country outing: fruits and vegetables, meats, cheeses, baked goods, wine. La Maseria de la Boqueria at the very back of the market specializes in cured and smoked meats, sausages, salamis, ham. Elsewhere, you'll also find dried fruits and sweets stands, even a chemist's, and of course a few tapas bars in case you need to fortify yourself for more shopping. Of these, Pinotxo (to your right from the main entrance) is the best bet with fine food that includes a house specialty of oysters with Cava. It's open from 6 am, so you can have a snack before you set out on the day's journey.

THEATRICAL BUILD-UP

14 Gran Teatre del Liceu

La Rambla, 51–59

The opera house that hosted the debut of Montserrat Caballé and decades of historic vocal performances burned to the ground in 1994 but the new theatre has won over opera lovers of all generations with its expanded design (the old Liceu had been overdue for expansion) and its lovingly recreated interiors. Red velvet and turn-of-the century style details imbue the new opera house with the glamour and nostalgic thrill of the old, legendary venue, but without the dust and the cracks and with the added benefits of modern building, lighting and sound technology.

BRIGHT AND BOLD

15 Carmelitas

Carrer del Doctor Dou, 1

The glowing red panels inserted between the old stone columns of the exterior announce a new presence here. Opened in early 2002, Carmelitas has caused a stir among Barcelonans who have become accustomed to the proliferation of new and trendy venues. The entrance feels like a stylish café-bar with white upholstered chairs and white formica tables grouped among white-painted Corinthian columns. Next door is a more formal restaurant space, though 'formal' here is not what your parents would call it. Downstairs is truly atmospheric: cavernous niches are filled with set tables and hung with theatrical red curtains, useful for large groups or just those desiring a little privacy. The menu is good, simple Catalan favourites: from *pa amb tomàquet* (bread rubbed with tomato) to fresh fish of the day and the bread and chocolate dessert.

ARTFUL BOOKS

16 Ras

Carrer del Doctor Dou, 10

Multidisciplinary architecture, design and publishing studio Actar is one of the forces behind this innovative gallery and exhibition space with a small but creatively designed bookshop. Actar are known for their cutting-edge book designs and the displays in the small shop area are as engaging as the artwork. International books on art, architecture, photography and design are set in curving polycarbonate shelves; magazines specializing in avant-garde fashion and design are cleverly arrayed behind transparent plastic netting.

FINE NEW FASHIONS

17 Giménez & Zuazo

162

BRIGHT YOUNG THING

18 Hostal Gat Raval

122

el cigaló
cordials

HIGH GLASS ARTS

19 Espai Vidre

Carrer dels Àngels, 8

Set coolly inside a converted industrial space that fits in well in the neighbourhood dominated by the Museu d'Art Contemporani de Barcelona (MACBA, see next page), the Espai Vidre is a gallery presenting new works by local and international artists in glass. These are highly inventive, original, one-off productions from the near-utilitarian, though exceedingly beautiful, forms of platters and bowls to large-scale sculpture. There is also a scheme for artists to attend workshops, make contact with other artists and develop exhibitions.

ARTISTIC ASIDES

20 Silenus

Carrer dels Àngels, 8

On the road to MACBA things have gone high design, but Silenus is a café-restaurant that despite a certain bid for style has kept things pretty comfortable. The fresco-style walls are hung with bits of arty objects but the overall atmosphere is relaxed. The menu is actually trying to do more than attract a few artistically inclined students, with some Barcelona classics like *llobarro costa amb arròs negre* (coastal sea bass with rice cooked in squid ink) and *calamars de platje amb faves* (squid served with broad beans), as well as pasta dishes and salads. The rooms play host to regular exhibitions of art.

THE ART OF JEWELRY

21 Forum Ferlandina

Carrer de Ferlandina, 31

Gallerist Beatriz Würsch opened this diminutive shop and gallery on the Plaça dels Àngels to help reinstate the place of jewelry in the world of art. She is also keen to promote the integration of the artistic programmes in the area, which with the building of MACBA has seen a creative explosion in recent years. Craftspeople can rent space in the workshop, which is next door to her very selective and well-designed shop space. She hosts exhibitions of work in other media, and the unique, one-off jewelry pieces sold here could sit just as well on a pedestal.

PERMANENT CONTEMPORARY

22 Museu d'Art Contemporani de Barcelona (MACBA)

Plaça dels Àngels, 1

This version of Richard Meier's signature white building is a refreshing addition to the Raval, putting contemporary art centre-stage within the city. Though its success in drawing top artists and eager crowds since 1995 has been less than originally hoped, the pleasing combination of natural light, user-friendly ramps and criss-crossing planes creates ideal exhibition spaces, which are gaining popularity with age. The current building, which was conceived in 1985, provided the first permanent home to the city's collection of contemporary art, which since 1969 had been housed in the Museu Víctor Balaguer in Vilanova i la Geltrú, so was a welcome addition anyway, and now with the Centre de Cultura Contemporània de Barcelona next door, it has created an artistic–cultural epicentre in the Raval.

MOTOWN
CASA ALMIRA
FUNDADA en 1860
La Paloma

DRINKS SINCE 1860

23 Casa Almirall

Carrer de Joaquín Costa, 33

The signage is a little patchy, but the Art Nouveau interior is still pretty much intact, complete with sweeping polished woodwork, carved with vegetal and floral motifs, and goddess torchères. The street was until recently considered seedy but since the installation of the MACBA brought a surge of youthful creative energy to this part of the Raval, the bar, opened in 1860, is finding a new generation of clients. However, like many old Barcelona spots, the Casa Almirall has always had a dedicated following and its appeal is a genuinely well-worn though very inspired atmosphere.

ARTISTIC EASE

24 Restaurant Plaça dels Àngels

Carrer de Ferlandina, 23

The open, paved plaza square was designed to be a meeting place for students and art lovers, however it is mostly occupied by daring skateboarders, who use Richard Meier's changing pavement levels to catapult themselves into all sorts of dynamic stunts. Close to the Carrer de Ferlandina, however, those artistic meetings are possible in the little cafés and shop/gallery spaces that have cropped up . The Restaurant Plaça dels Àngels is one of the best, with an admirably eclectic interior, reasonably priced café-bar offerings, terrace seating outside and that creative youthful ambience inside.

OLD SPANISH STYLE

25 Hotel Meson Castilla

118

DANCE HALL DAYS

26 La Paloma

Carrer del Tigre, 27

A giant-sized yellow frontage with red shutters and a large dove made of fairy lights is the sign for this early 1900s dance hall, which retains its Baroque ornament as well as its devotees. From 6 to 9:30 in the evenings from Thursday to Saturday it's all ballroom, with a live orchestra playing classic dance numbers for the middle-aged and older crowd. Then it closes its polite doors and re-opens as a DJ club. Thursdays it's presided over by DJ-duo the Dope brothers (De Lippo and Professor Angel Dust, see Oven, p. 57), who play funk, house and Afro-Latino. A dance-hall experience for all generations and tastes.

ON SECOND-HAND ROW

27 Carrer de la Riera Baixa

- Lailo, no. 20
- Zero, no. 12
- Erretè, no. 10
- wah wah, no. 14
- Edison's, no. 9&10

A small alleyway of delights for the second-hand or vintage fanatic, the Carrer de la Riera Baixa has become a mecca for those on the search for non-standard used goods and collector's pieces. The largest cache among a cooperative group of nearly two dozen shops is at Lailo, where Anna Vizcaino, daughter of the shop's founder, presides over rooms of second-hand, vintage designer, theatrical and antique wedding apparel. The immaculate leather and denim items at the front are only the tip of the iceberg, for there are rooms at the back, downstairs and up filled with sartorial treasures. Artists, writers and designers come here to rent one of the costumes from the Liceu production of *Carmen* so that they can copy a pattern or stitching. Video and TV producers come for the vintage 1920s, '30s and '40s dresses and suits or some of her vast store of theatrical period clothing, all of which is kept in top condition. Not everything is so rarefied: the shop entrance is jammed with affordable second-hand items that manage to look incredibly trendy. Also look out for fetish and techno gear at Zero, new street design by the independent label Erretè, and vintage CDs of the 1960s and '70s – psychedelia, easy-listening, West Coast, blues – at wah wah. Edison's is for the vinyl lover of all ages, but also carries an eclectic range of CDs, cassettes and singles.

HAPHAZARD HARMONY

28 Merry Ant

156

CAUSING A STIR

29 Colibrí

Carrer de la Riera Alta, 33–35

A new restaurant that does classic dishes with creative flair, Colibri is winning friends and influencing cuisine under the guidance of César and Remedios Pastor. Monkfish, that Catalan favourite, is sliced up and served in pine-nut vinaigrette; salad of potatoes with prawns is elevated to a new status with truffle-Chardonnay dressing. These and pigeon cooked with its own pâté are some of the exciting courses coming from César's carefully orchestrated kitchen, while Remedios ensures the desserts are definitely something to write home about.

FINE OLD-FASHIONED

30 Casa Leopoldo

130

BOOKS AND COINS UNDER A MODERNISTA ROOF

31 Mercat de Sant Antoni

Between Carrer de Tamarit and Carrer de Manso

The pretty Modernista structure was designed (1876–82) by Antoni Rovira i Trias and engineer Josep M. Cornet i Mas (also partly responsible for the market of El Born, p. 53). During the week it houses a fruit and vegetable market. On Sundays, however, the specialists take over, with second-hand and antique books and coins filling up the stall spaces. There is a lot to look at even if you're not up to purchasing anything: from the fine, leatherbound volumes to dimestore novels, magazines and comic books and coins of all varieties. The market is open from 10 am until 2 pm.

SIMPLE PLEASURES

32 La Parra

Carrer de Joanot Martorell, 3

Rustic doesn't begin to describe the patchy plaster, the rough stone and simple crockery of this well-kept country-style outpost near the Sants district northwest of the Raval. The welcoming interior has all the charm of a 19th-century inn, while outdoors, a vine-covered terrace provides a pastoral vignette. Hearty, stew-based dishes and a variety of meats cooked over a wood flame and served traditionally plain with an ample dollop of *allioli* (the classic Catalan accompaniment of olive oil creamed together with crushed garlic) are wholly in keeping with the idyllic peasant ambience. Don't expect anything too delicate, and you will be well and fully satisfied.

ART PARK

33 Parc Joan Miró (Parc de l'Escorxador)

At the corner of Carrer d'Aragó and Carrer de Tarragona

It is to the city's credit that even before the Olympic building frenzy a host of urban-development projects created public parks and pedestrian squares. Among the larger and more successful schemes is the Parc Joan Miró, which is hailed by Miró's towering *Dona i Ocell* ('Woman and Bird') overlooking a reflecting pool and paved and planted areas alternating in four city blocks of open space. Nearby, just below the Sants rail station on a former industrial site, is also the fantastical Parc de l'Espanya Industrial, with its intriguing towers and dragon sculpture.

Marie
Brizard
Ron
Pujol
Fenimore
MARK
TWAIN

INVENTING MINIMALISM

34 Pavelló Barcelona

Avinguda del Marquès de Comillas

Probably one of the most influential buildings of the 20th century, Ludwig Mies van der Rohe's pavilion designed for the Barcelona Exhibition of 1929 was a harbinger of the Modern movement, with its pristine intersecting planes and focus on materials and surfaces over ornament. Rectangles of glass and marble articulate space without enclosing it, much as the roof projects well beyond the walls so that the whole concept of house building is exploded or rather elegantly reformed. Rectangular reflecting pools continue the play of geometry and surfaces in an eloquent justification of 'less is more'. The original pavilion was destroyed after the exhibition, but this 1986 meticulous reconstruction perfectly re-creates the true essence of the Modern.

HILLTOP CULTURE

35 Montjuïc

- Castell de Montjuïc
- Museu Nacional d'Art de Catalunya
- Jardins de Mossèn Costa i Llobera
- Jardí Botànic

Montjuïc is the name for the mountainous and largely unpopulated area south of the city centre, which is home to Barcelona's 17th-century Castell, a fortress occupied by the military until the 1960s. Happily, Montjuïc's association with militaristic vigilance has since been superseded by cultural and ecological interests. Reached by funicular, it is now covered with a number of venues built for the 1992 summer Olympics, as well as green spaces, both landscaped and semi-wild. It is also a cultural park of theatre venues and museums, the most fascinating historical space being the Museu Nacional d'Art de Catalunya, located in the Palau Nacional and housing the world's finest collection of Romanesque frescoes. The castle is now home to the Museu Militar and can be reached by the cable cars (Teleferic) running from the funicular station. Below it, within the triangular loop of the Carretera de Miramar, are some of the more exotic gardens of Montjuïc, the Jardins de Mossèn Costa i Llobera, which are planted with a range of tropical plants and a variety of cactus species in gloriously colourful bunches, all of which seem quite at home on the coastal hillside. The very different landscapes (and sea views) of the Jardins del Mirador and Jardins de Mossèn Cinto Verdaguer are uphill from here, while just below the Olympic Stadium is the Jardí Botànic (completed 2001) with its low-lying, zigzagging buildings set amid grass-covered triangular berms and beds that produce a modern mosaic of flora.

CATALAN MODERN

36 Fundació Joan Miró

Parc de Montjuïc

Bounded by another of Montjuïc's bountiful gardens on one side, the Jardins de la Ribal, and by the Teatre Grec on another, the Fundació Joan Miró is also close to the funicular station that brings you up the mountain the easy way. A native of Barcelona, Miró developed the idea of a foundation to receive his works, and those of other artists, with architect Josep Lluís Sert. Sert created the striking white building in 1975 using a highly modern design for exhibitions with plenty of clean white space and natural light. An extension was added by Jaume Freixa in 1986, but the building adheres to Sert's original plan of rooms centred around interior and exterior courtyards, with Catalan elements like tiles and vaulting subtly interwoven. Its timeless quality was confirmed when it was given the 'Twenty-Five-Year Award' by the American Institute of Architects in 2002. A roof terrace provides a display space for some of Miró's vividly painted sculpture and an opportunity to take advantage of the hilltop views. The permanent collection includes works from all periods in painting, ceramics and textiles (from the early Fauvist and the Surrealist to the dark Civil War and postwar works to his later experimentation). Rounding out the comprehensive collection are pieces by Miró's contemporaries: Alexander Calder (his Mercury Fountain created for the World Fair of 1937), Henry Moore, Fernand Léger, Marcel Duchamp and Max Ernst. The Espai 13 is a popular exhibition space devoted to contemporary artists. A café and restaurant provide the much-needed refreshment to fortify you for trekking around the mountain.

Eixample

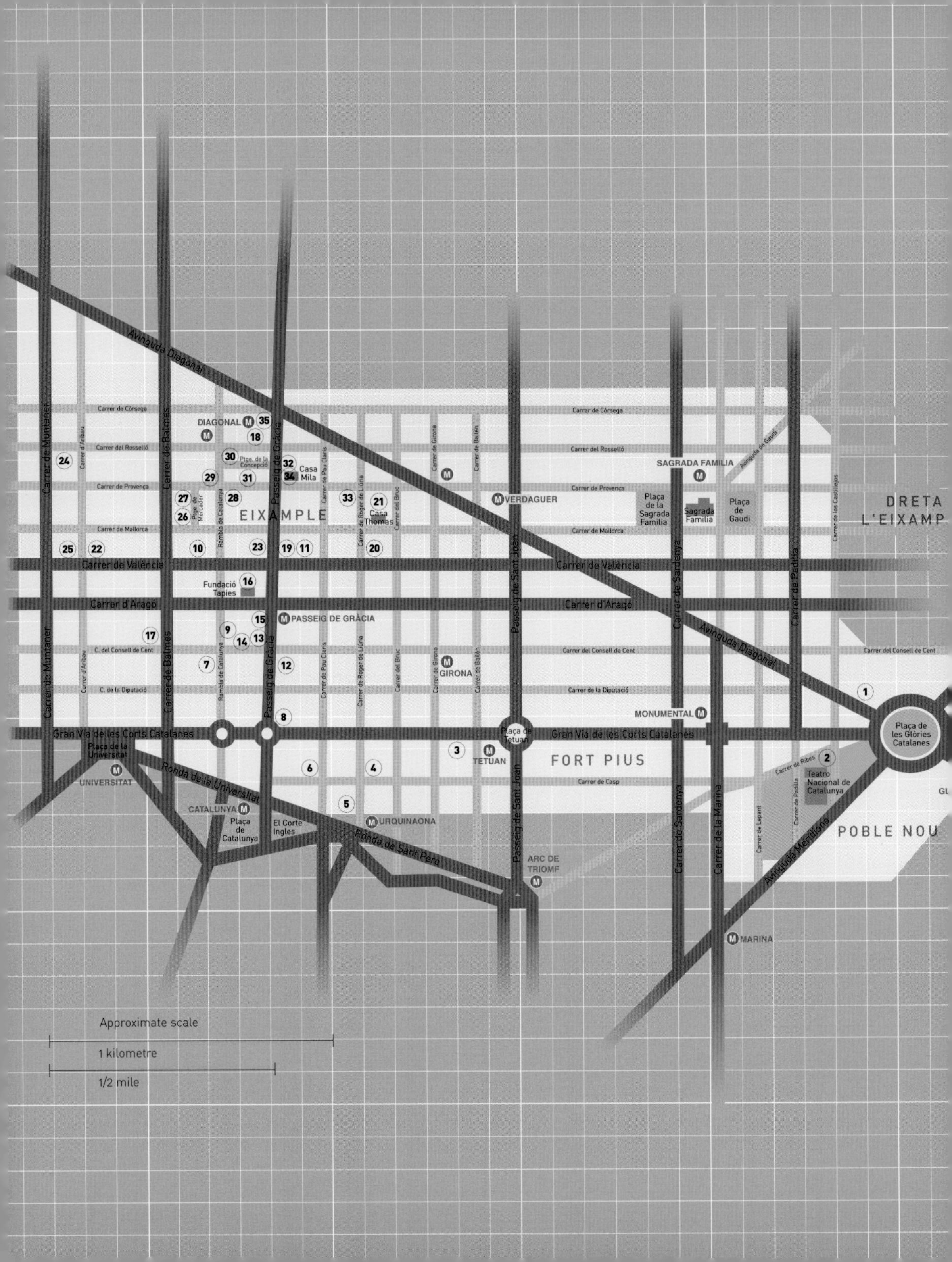

Avinguda Diagonal
Carrer de Muntaner
Carrer de Balmes
Passeig de Gràcia
Carrer de Còrsega
Carrer del Rosselló
Carrer de Provença
Carrer de Mallorca
Carrer de València
Carrer d'Aragó
C. del Consell de Cent
C. de la Diputació
Gran Via de les Corts Catalanes
Carrer d'Aribau
Rambla de Catalunya
Ptge. de Mercader
Ptge. de la Concepció
Carrer de Pau Claris
Carrer de Roger de Llúria
Carrer del Bruc
Carrer de Girona
Carrer de Bailèn
Passeig de Sant Joan
Carrer de Sardenya
Carrer de la Marina
Carrer de Padilla
Carrer de los Castillejos
Avinguda de Gaudí
Carrer del Consell de Cent
Carrer de la Diputació
Carrer de Casp
Carrer de Ribes
Carrer de Lepant
Avinguda Meridiana
Ronda de la Universitat
Ronda de Sant Pere
DIAGONAL
Casa Mila
EIXAMPLE
Casa Thomas
Fundació Tapies
PASSEIG DE GRÀCIA
GIRONA
VERDAGUER
SAGRADA FAMILIA
Plaça de la Sagrada Familia
Sagrada Familia
Plaça de Gaudi
DRETA L'EIXAMP
MONUMENTAL
Plaça de Tetuan
TETUAN
FORT PIUS
Plaça de les Glòries Catalanes
Teatro Nacional de Catalunya
POBLE NOU
Plaça de la Universitat
UNIVERSITAT
CATALUNYA
Plaça de Catalunya
El Corte Ingles
URQUINAONA
ARC DE TRIOMF
MARINA
Approximate scale
1 kilometre
1/2 mile

Before the great Olympic regeneration project of the 1990s, the last large-scale improvements to Barcelona were carried out when the Eixample ('enlargement') was created in the 1860s and extended the city limits of Barcelona into the surrounding villages of Horta, Les Corts, Gràcia, Sant Gervasi and Sarrià. Ildefons Cerdà won the competition to expand the city from the Ciutat Vella with a grid system that wraps around the old city and spreads northwest in the grand avenues of the Diagonal, the Gran Via de les Corts Catalanes and the Meridiana. His original scheme involved regular interventions of green space and was meant to be thoroughly democratic, with no single neighbourhood or street better than the rest. In the event, Cerdà's vision was not built strictly to plan, so that while in some ways the Eixample became more urban sprawl than social utopia, it did pave the way, quite literally, for the construction of some of Barcelona's, if not Europe's, most distinctive 20th-century architectural achievements.

One possible itinerary begins at the bottom of the Eixample with Gaudí's Casa Calvet, which has been for many years an upscale restaurant (p. 134). Further up the Passeig de Gràcia, Modernista landmarks appear: Josep Puig i Cadafalch's Dutch-style Casa Amatller next to Gaudí's exuberant Casa Batlló (p. 86); the Fundació Antoni Tàpies (p. 87) set up by the Catalan artist in a former publishing house designed by Domènech i Montaner; the design firm BD Ediciones housed in Domènech i Montaner's Casa Thomas. Back along the Passeig de Gràcia is the Casa Milà (p. 93), which went through serious neglect but was rescued by the Caixa de Catalunya. Here from the roof, Gaudí's unfinished masterwork, the Sagrada Familia can be seen in the distance rising like a stalwart reminder of the architect's vision.

In addition to providing a setting for these masterworks, Passeig de Gràcia became a sort of triumphal parade of expensive shops and residences, and it continues to reflect the upper echelons of Barcelona consumerism and style, largely dominated by international labels. Whereas some of the city's most ground-breaking restaurants and streetwear designers have set up in the Ribera or the Raval, the high-fashion names, haute-cuisine establishments and art galleries are set firmly in the luxury-lined premises along and near this grand boulevard, where even the paving stones show attention to design. It is hard not to feel that the grand axis of the Passeig de Gràcia and the great sweep of the Diagonal resemble the processional avenues of much larger and once-imperial international cities. That they exist in Barcelona and to such glorious effect is a tribute to how much this city has packed inside it.

SECOND-HAND AND GRAND

1 Mercat Encants Vells

Dos de Maig, 186

In an area northwest of the huge road interchange at the Plaça de les Glòries (between Carrer dos de Maig and Carrer de Cartagena) is probably Barcelona's largest and most varied flea market. Antique furnishings, second-hand clothing, tools, vintage items and of course a lot of less obvious 'treasures' are bursting from hundreds of stalls. If you come by underground don't be confused by the fringe 'market' that spreads out into the little nearby park where dozens lay the contents of their closets out on the ground. If you go by taxi, ask the driver; the place is well-marked in large red letters and organized in sections of stalls. It's prime pick-pocketing ground, so guard your belongings as you sift through the goods on offer. Mornings are best.

DRAMATIC ARTS

2 Teatre Nacional de Catalunya

Plaça de les Arts, 1

Near the flea market, along the Avenguda Meridiana (you'll want a taxi from the market), is one of Barcelona's grandest – and to some, its most ostentatious – building projects of the last ten years, the Teatre Nacional de Catalunya, built by local architect Ricardo Bofill in a style that looks like a replica of the Pantheon but with acres of glass walls and skylighting. It opened to divided opinion in 1997, but with three venues, the theatre offers a range of productions, recently works by Kafka and Molière alternating with modern Spanish productions. The grand atrium space includes a formal restaurant.

CHAMPAGNE WISHES...

3 La Bodegueta del Xampú

Gran Via de les Corts Catalanes, 702

The Catalans like their Cava and they like their snacks made of regional 'artisanal' produce almost as much. At Xampú, corn-fed cured hams, home-made cheeses, tinned oysters, sardines, farmhouse-style preserves and all manner of foie gras are sold packaged or served as *platillos* to taste alongside the daily offerings of champagnes and wines by the glass. The sparkling stuff is not limited to the Catalan or even Spanish varieties, so taste-test at your leisure.

MY DINNER WITH GAUDÍ

4 Casa Calvet

134

PERUCCHI
CERDO
La Jabugueña
JABUGO

J. ROCA

FABRICS WITH FLAIR

5 Casals Pagès

Carrer de Roger de Llúria, 7

This is the latest outlet for the fabric empire of Ribes and Casals who opened their first shop in 1933, which moved to its current location in 1945. Casals Pagès is an updated showroom for the venerable traders that gives them ample space to display their tremendous range of silks, wools, cottons and embroidered, appliquéed and finely woven fabrics that range from everyday use to fabrics for 'carnival and spectacle' and 'fantasy'. For your own creative ideas or for something to surprise your dressmaker or upholsterer, have a rifle through the bolts on the tables and walls or talk to one of the numerous helpful assistants.

FOR LITERARY APPETITES

6 Laie

Carrer de Pau Claris, 85

With the proliferation some years ago of the bookshop-cafés that attended to neither aspect very well, it is nice to see someone trying to do both and succeeding. The downstairs bookshop is well stocked and well organized. A knowledgeable selection of literary fiction titles in English appears at the front near a good range of magazines. Beyond are fiction and non-fiction in Spanish with art and architecture towards the back. They pride themselves on finding you the book you want (or, as they say, 'the one you didn't know you wanted') and so go out of their way to help. Upstairs, the café is no mere addendum, it's a warm, wood-lined space with lots of plants, good lighting and a varied menu for breakfast, lunch and dinner. Laie also hosts frequent lectures and readings.

EXOTIC CHOCOLATES

7 Cacao Sampaka

175

GENERATIONS OF JEWELS

8 J. Roca

Passeig de Gràcia, 18

Josep Lluís Sert designed these premises for the family firm of J. Roca in 1933, but not everyone appreciated his progressive approach since it replaced a café designed by Gaudí. However, the building, like the jewellers, has only become more revered over time. Roca has been around for over a century, so their designs tend towards a traditional sort of elegance, though some of the 'mosaic' pieces have both an Art Deco/vintage and modern appeal. A collection 'Gaudí' takes inspiration from designs and patterns of the Casa Milà and the Parc Güell. See their recently redesigned shop at Diagonal, 580, for a look at their take on a more modern, 'minimalist' style.

PATRONS OF ART

9 Galeria Joan Prats

Rambla de Catalunya, 54

The stained-glass façade gives a date of 1845, but it was taken from another shop when Josep Lluís Sert converted these premises to gallery space in 1976. The owners, Manuel and Joan de Muga, named this gallery for the proprietor of the hat shop formerly at this location. However, Joan Prats (1891–1970) was known as much for his patronage of Catalan culture and his friendship with artists such as Antoni Tàpies, Joan Miró and Picasso as for his custom-made hats. The gallery was started with the idea of promoting local artists like Ràfols Casamada, Hernandez Pijuan and Guinovart but soon became involved with works by Picasso, Miró and Max Ernst. Wilfredo Lam, Christo, Robert Motherwell and Sue Williams are among the international artists who have shown here recently in addition to Spain's Eduardo Chillida, Pablo Palazuelo and Juan Uslé.

MASTERFULLY WOVEN

10 David Valls

169

WE SHOULD ALL HAVE THEM

11 Bad Habits

171

SILKY ELEGANCE

12 Antonio Pernas

Carrer del Consell de Cent, 314–16

Antonio Pernas, based in his native La Coruña, has risen to become, along with names like Roberto Verino, an ambassador of Spanish fashion. His clothes are streamlined with minimal decoration and each season is in a limited palette of carefully matched colours that includes browns and turquoise toned with grey, as well as dark red. But then there are some nice surprises: a neatly cut double-breasted corduroy coat done in bold grape, for example, or, for his lines in white satin in an array of tailored cuts. His look is long, lean, often cinched at the waist for an elegant, tailored look. His collection includes shoes, suits and evening wear but the shop shows primarily his sophisticated daywear.

ART NOUVEAU JEWELRY

13 Bagués Masriera

166

FASHION FAVOURITE

14 Antonio Miro

168

FLIGHTS OF FANCY

15 Casa Batlló

Passeig de Gràcia, 43

Juxtaposed with the Casa Amatller, built by Josep Puig i Cadafalch in 1900, the Casa Batlló, designed by Antoni Gaudí with Josep Jujol and completed in 1907, demonstrates Gaudí's unique contribution to the Modernista movement. Actually a remodel of an existing building (1877) for a distinguished textile-producing family, the Casa Batlló design had to contend with Puig i Cadafalch's spirited façade next door without seeming to compete. Gaudí has left behind those Mudéjar geometries that he embraced in the Casa Vicens (p. 103) and which are echoed in the Dutch-style stepped façade of the Casa Amatller, and given free reign to the organic forms that would later distinguish the Casa Milà (p. 93). Both Gaudí exteriors have been smoothed and shaped to the point where they resemble sculpted marshmallow rather than cold hard stone. The Batlló's protruding bays, coloured mosaics and stained-glass windows add elements of sheer fantasy, adamantly defying the gravity, uniformity and dullness of the urban landscape.

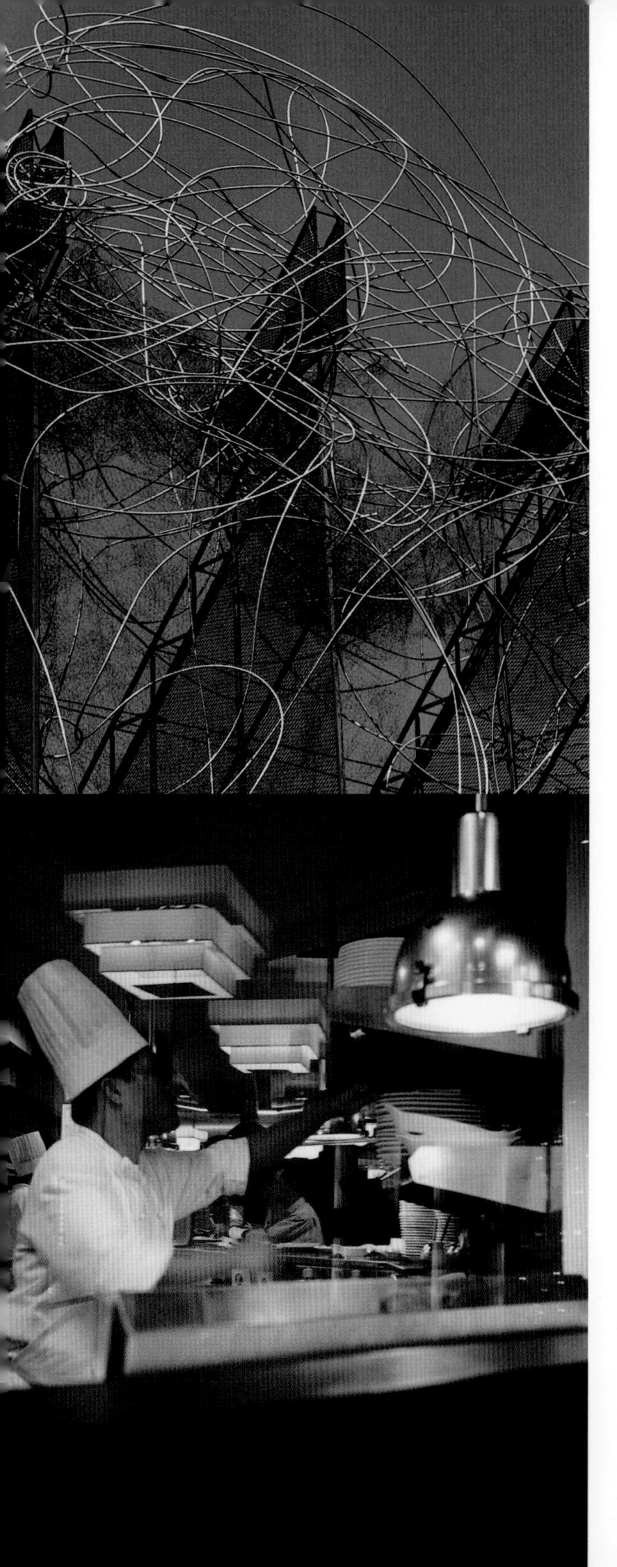

MODERNISTA SPACE FOR MODERN ARTIST

16 Fundació Antoni Tàpies

Carrer d'Aragó, 255

Catalan painter Antoni Tàpies (b. 1923), one of the most important living Spanish artists, was initially attracted to the surrealism of the Dau al Set group but later branched out to make a name for himself with his abstract forms that experimented with textures in paint and mixed media. His foundation was created to promote 'the study and understanding of modern art and culture'. Its home is an 1885 Modernista structure originally designed by Domènech i Montaner for a publishing company, its brick and iron enlivened with Moorish decoration and Tàpies's own *Núvol i Cadira* (Cloud and Chair) metal sculpture floating like a mesh scribble above. Inside, the loft-like space was remodelled by Lluis Domènech Girbau and Roser Amadó in 1989 to hold the permanent collections and exhibition space. This is the place to find the most complete collection of Tàpies's own work held anywhere and in an appropriately Catalan context, as well as modern and contemporary art from around the world. The building also houses an art research centre and library, and there is a well-stocked bookshop.

CALM AND CLASSIC

17 L'Olive

Carrer de Balmes, 47

There are a number of very good restaurants dotted around the Eixample and L'Olive is one of them. It is no Modernista gem, rather it is a well-designed modern restaurant with décor (largely dark greens and dark wood) that is as discreet and mature as its service. You'll find a number of businessmen here for lunch, but also families. The menu announces 'Mediterranean Catalan Cuisine' (and can be had in languages other than Spanish and Catalan), which means overall a lighter approach to traditional cooking. For example, a native staple, *sopa de peix i marisc* (fish soup), is a bowl of clear dark broth with tender chunks of white fish and substantial pieces of prawns, both the salt and the fish flavours kept to a very palatable margin. The fish and beef dishes are very simple indeed, such as the *sepietes amb all i julivert* (cuttlefish in garlic and parsley) served only with a bit of tender potato to soak up the excess. Desserts include one of the lightest *crema Catalanas* you'll find anywhere.

MADRID GEMS

18 Joaquín Berao

Carrer del Rosselló, 277

Berao is a Madrid-based designer, but his Barcelona premises are a good port of call for jewelry hounds. Since the beginning of his career in 1982 his sweeping, organic pieces and geometric forms have been both popular and highly regarded in the fashion press. He was awarded the Prince Felipe prize in 2002 for his pioneering work in Spanish jewelry design. This outlet, designed by Tonet Sunyer (also responsible for the new flower stalls on the Ramblas de les Flors) and Tomàs Morató, is a lesson in art and architecture on a small scale.

HIGH ROMANCE

19 Drolma

135

BARCELONA DESIGN

20 Roser i Francesc

Carrer de València, 285

Though it's one of those near-hidden places, partially below ground, it has the look of an established Eixample clothes shop – clean, elegant, refined – with polished wood floors and tidy displays. However, the stock is markedly more interesting than the more traditional offerings along the Passeig de Gràcia. Here you'll find innovative designs for men and women produced under Roser Francesc's own label as well as collections by David Valls, Antonio Miro and other independent Spanish designers.

HOME OF DESIGN

21 BD: Ediciones de Diseño

172

GOURMET TO TAKE AWAY

22 Halagos

Carrer de València, 189

The name means 'pleasures' or 'delights', which is what Maite Leucía provides in her prettily packaged shop selling gourmet produce. As you might have noticed from the restaurant menus, the Catalans have quite a fondness for 'foie', that is, Catalan-style goose-, duck- or chicken-liver pâté, and Halagos has a large selection of its own brand, with variations such as 'cassoulet confit', 'mousse au foie' and 'fritton'. While Leucía carries a number of French products, many of the wines, liqueurs, cheeses, hams and preserves are from Catalonia or other Spanish regions.

MODERNISTA STYLE

23 Hotel Condes de Barcelona

124

NOUVELLE EXOTIC

24 Semproniana

Carrer del Rosselló, 148

Opened in 1993 by chef/proprietor Ada Parellada, Semproniana had an early start on the new wave of Barcelona design-happy restaurants offering a mix of traditional and new cuisine. Architect Santiago Alegre helped convert the former printworks but Parellada herself bestowed the décor, a mix of exotic romance with dark pink walls, swags of gauzy drapery and an array of tapestry fabrics. The service could be a little more friendly and the menu (Catalan/Spanish with a twist) seems more quirky than necessary, but it all comes together to gratify the senses. The lasagne with *butifarra negra* is, in more ways than one, a case in point.

MODERN WINE AND TAPAS

25 CATA 1.81

154

SERIOUS ABOUT PHOTOGRAPHY

26 Kowasa Gallery

Carrer de Mallorca, 235

Kowasa Gallery opened in 1992 with the aim of offering the best selection of books on photography in Europe. They also carry books on art, architecture and design, with special photography sections for travel, nature, fashion, photojournalism and early photography. As a sign of just how serious they are about the art, they set up a gallery space in 1997 devoted to modern and historic Spanish photography, holding regular exhibitions of the medium that feature work from its beginnings to the present day. They also hold their own archive of international and Spanish photography, the latter including some fascinating and rare images from the Civil War.

DESIGNED FOR ART

27 Galería Estrany de la Mota

Passatge de Mercader, 18

One of Europe's most prestigious and innovative galleries is set in a quiet, patrician street off the main thoroughfares of the Eixample. With a reputation for presenting some of Spain's biggest names, it has every reason to look smug, which, from the outside, it does. It also looks very cool, contemporary and authoritative, which partly belies its focus on cutting-edge and experimental work. Pep Agut, Antoni Abad, Thomas Ruff and Jean-Marc Bustamante are represented here, and changing exhibitions feature new native and international artists.

CATALAN CHIC

28 Principal

133

AVANT-GARDE DESIGN OUTLET

29 Hipòtesi

167

ARTISANAL LEATHER

30 Muxart

165

QUICK SUCCESSION

31 Tragaluz and Tragarapid

Passatge de la Concepció, 5

This is an early venture by the Grupo Tragaluz (see also Principal, p. 133), which came to be defined by the grand glass ceiling and skylight (*tragaluz*) in the upstairs dining area that is an indoor terrace garden of many delights. Sandra Tarruella's and Pepe Cortés's award-winning interiors and Javier Mariscal's graphic contributions, which include the menu design, made Tragaluz the place to see and be seen when it opened in 1990. It has lost little of its appeal, with a hip downstairs bar area serving quick meals (Tragrapid) and the restaurant turning out highly acclaimed fusion dishes with practised elegance. Monkfish in black olive and tomato confit is one of the modernized traditional dishes. Try the 'chocolate in three textures' for dessert. The Tragaluz team are also responsible for the restaurant El Japonés across the road at no. 2.

DESIGN ORIGINALS

32 Vinçon

Passeig de Gràcia, 96

At first glance, Vinçon looks like another late-century design emporium like Habitat. It does carry the ubiquitous international design names but, having been on the scene since 1941 and occupying a historic building designed in 1899 by Josep Rovira Rabassa, Vinçon has long been a design icon (the bags are regularly redesigned by known artists and are very popular) and offers some uniquely Spanish creations at reasonable prices. Owner Fernando Amat, a well-known figure in the Barcelona design world, is the man at the helm of this vast collection. Some notable Spanish designs include lighting, of course, for which they seem to have a particular flair, and some lines of ceramics, like the subtle blue-and-white geometric patterns by Aguadé and Aramis as well as matching glassware by Vidreco, are things you won't find easily elsewhere. Even if you don't want to ship anything back, the first-floor furniture gallery is worth a look as it spills out on to a terrace offering close views of La Pedrera (p. 93).

BEYOND BAROQUE

33 Josep Font

GAUDÍ REDUX

34 Casa Milà/La Pedrera

Passeig de Gràcia, 92

The Caixa de Catalunya savings bank purchased the building originally designed by Antoni Gaudí for the Milà family (1906–11). Like many of Barcelona's Modernista gems, the Casa Milà had been sadly neglected and was ridiculed as 'the stone quarry' (La Pedrera) before the bank started refurbishment work in 1991. Now the courtyard is open, affording a view of Gaudí's voluptuously curving spaces, and in the attic, now the Espai Gaudí, the only comprehensive exhibition of the architect's work and life has been laid out in a recent restoration that cleared away later apartment divisions to reveal Gaudi's original Gothic-style interior. On the roof terrace, chimneys added later and obstructions have been removed and a new walkway, a series of up-and-down steps, allows visitors to see up close the sculptural wonderland that is the Gaudí signature (you can even have drinks up here in the summer months, see p. 155). On the fourth floor is a reconstruction of the early-20th-century bourgeois apartment rooms, ending in a surprisingly enticing period-themed shop.

CATALAN EXPO

35 Palau Robert

Passeig de Gràcia, 107

In another celebration of Catalan heritage, this 19th-century neoclassical-style building was made over in 1997 as a tourist information office (Centre d'Informació de Catalunya) and space for exhibitions on themes of Catalan art and culture. In addition to longer-term art exhibits, the Palau also has regular concerts and every month and a half hosts a gastronomic presentation focusing on one of Catalonia's most distinguished chefs. Past participants have included Ferran Adrià, currently the culinary sensation behind El Bulli (p. 180), and Xavier Pellicer, who opened Abac (p. 132) in 2000 and quickly earned a Michelin star there. A small bookshop is situated on the ground floor, and entrance to the Palau gives you access to the oasis-like, palm-filled courtyard garden behind.

Gràcia
Zona Alta

TIBIDABO
SANT JUST DESVERN
29
Funicular al Tibidabo
Parc Font del Racó
Plaça del Funicular
28
Plaça del Doctor Andreu
Tramvia Blau
SARRIÀ
33
Museu Monestir de Pedralbes
27
Plaça de John F. Kennedy
26
Passeig de la Bonanova
Plaça de la Bonanova
AVINGUDA TIBIDABO
SARRIÀ
Carrer de Pau Alcover
BONANOVA
SANT GERVASI DE CASSOLES
VALLCARCA
Ronda del General Mitre
LA BONANOVA
Via Augusta
Gran Via de Carles III
Avinguda Diagonal
MARIA CRISTINA
Plaça de Prat de la Riba
22
C. de Sant Elies
Plaça Lesseps
LESSEPS
GRACIA
Travessera de Dalt
13
Casa Vicens
FONTANA
7
5
Plaça de la Virreina
8
4
C. del Montseny Perla
14
10
9
6
JOANIC
Travessera de Gràcia
3
2
1
C. de Còrsega
EIXAMPLE
24
24
25
Jardins del Poeta E. Marquina
23
21
C.de Laforja
19
C. de l'Avenir
20
Trav. de Gràcia
17
16
18
15
12
11
Carrer de la Indústria
Carrer de Còrsega
Carrer de Pau Claris
Passeig de Gràcia
Rambla de Catalunya
Carrer de Bailen
Passeig de Sant Joan
MONTBAU
MUNDET
MONTBAU
VALL D'HEBRON
31
Parc La Clota
Parc la Crueta del Coll
Parc Güell
32
CARMEL
HORTA
30
Parc del Guinardó
GUINARDÓ
Avinguda de l'Estatut de Catalunya
Ronda del Guinardó
ALFONS X
GUINARDÓ
Hospital de la Santa Creu i de Sant Pau
Carrer de Sant Antoni Maria Claret
CAMP DE L'ARPA
Avinguda Diagonal
Approximate scale
1 kilometre
1/2 mile

The urban scale reduces noticeably northwest of the Eixample, where the Passeig de Gràcia begins to constrict into the Carrer Gran de Gràcia. One of many villages brought into the municipal fold with the creation of the Eixample, Gràcia is traversed by a thicket of mainly single-lane streets, punctuated by *plaças* surrounded by shops and small pavement cafés that happily retain its village character. A programme of refurbishment in the 1980s pedestrianized the squares, moving traffic around and parking sometimes underground, and added thoughtfully designed street furniture and trees, as in the Plaça del Sol (p. 100), which has become a lively spot for drinking and dining during sunny afternoons and for friends meeting up in the balmy evenings. The Modernista character in this part of the city is toned down: façades more often have delicate painted or cast decoration than boldly curving organic forms. Gaudí's first major commission, Casa Viçens (p. 103), however, is an architectural style of its own.

The regeneration of the squares of Gràcia marked a larger wave of popularity in the last few years which has brought new visitors to the cafés and small ethnic restaurants for which the neighbourhood has been known. Enterprising designers and shopkeepers are opening a particularly Gràcian brand of unique boutiques, and two of the biggest names in Barcelona design – Lydia Delgado in fashion (p. 169) and Jaume Tresserra in furniture (p. 108) – have their shops and showrooms here. As well as having a wealth of cafés, Gràcia is also home to a long list of outstanding restaurants both new and well-established. From the intimate appeal of Ot (p. 142) to the haute cusine of Jean-Luc Figueras (p. 144), from the discreet luxury of Roig Robi (p. 144) to the bold innovation of El Raco d'en Freixa (p. 145), this little neighbourhood is a dense microcosm of Catalan cuisine. Crowning these creative and epicurean splendours to the north is Gaudí's breathtaking Parc Güell.

Beyond the village charms of Gràcia, the higher altitude of the Zona Alta beckons. To the west, in Sant Just Desvern, where Ricardo Bofill created his controversial housing development Walden 7 in the 1970s, creative types of another kind built a nightclub-restaurant that takes Bofill's futuristic tendencies a bit further (see Walden 8, p. 108). East of this outlying suburb, the monastery of Pedralbes has become a backdrop of solemn splendour for the Thyssen Bornemisza collection of medieval art. Restaurants like La Venta (see p. 131) and La Balsa (p. 108) combine a leafy, hillside settings and spectacular views over the city with dining that is set apart from the masses, providing moments to savour, day or night.

EL GLOP
-Broxeta de rap i llagostins
-Espaguetis carbonara
-Provolone
-Filet de vedella a l'oporto
-Lluç a la basca
-Carpaccio de salmó i bacallà
-Orada o llobarro al forn

SWEETNESS AND LIGHT

1 Xurreria Trebol

Carrer de Córsega, 341

You can't sit down, there isn't even a bar. This little slice of *churro* heaven straddling the border of the Eixample is purely take-away, but the *churros* (plain or filled with cream, *dulce de leche*) and little cakes with *cabellos de ángel* (thin, sweet vermicelli) at the Trebol are so good you would finish them before you sat down anyway. Since 1952 the churreria has been supplying afternoon sustenance for the amblers around the Carrer de Córsega and Passeig de Gràcia. And if you wander down a few metres you can have a good long look at no. 316, the Casa Comalat (by Salvador Valeri i Pupurull, 1911) in all its pink-and-green Modernista glory as you crunch the perfect *churro* – crunchy and sugary on the outside, soft and doughy on the inside.

THE NAME OF HAUTE CUISINE

2 Jean Luc Figueras

144

A GOURMET PALETTE

3 Ot

142

HOME-COOKED FAVOURITES

4 Taverna El Glop

Carrer de Montmany, 46

It certainly has the feel of a well-loved taverna, with low ceilings, wood beams, checked tablecloths and signed photos on the walls. The conservatory-style downstairs space also fills up with people coming for the hearty stews and grilled meat and fish dishes, the pitchers of regional wine and the homey atmosphere. Daily specials range from salmon ravioli to monkfish and shrimp brochette and baked sea bass.

CAFÉ PLACES

5 Plaça de la Virreina

Another square redesigned by Bach and Mora (see Plaça del Sol, p. 100) to improve pedestrian access is bordered on the north by the church of St Joan, with its boldly incongruous mosaic signage contrasting with the centuries-old façade and on the south by the rectilinear tower marking the top of Carrer de Torrijos. The plaça is lined with cafés; great for a quiet afternoon snack or drink outdoors.

CLEAN, WELL-LIGHTED PLACE

6 Café Salambo

Carrer de Torrijos, 51

Towards the end of the day the children go home and the promenading types meander from the Carrer d'Asturies and down the Torrijos, which is lined with interesting shops and cafés, of which Salambo, a café-bar, has to be one of the most appealing in the Gràcia area. The ground floor is an inviting space with scrolled iroko wood benches attracting those who come to read and those who come to sip and talk. Upstairs are more tables and another bar serving good snacks, tapas, wine and hot drinks.

CATALAN IRAQI CUISINE

7 Mesopotamia

Carrer de Verdi, 65

Just west of the Plaça de la Virreina is one of Gràcia's (and Barcelona's) more exotic treats. Mesopotamia is an Iraqi restaurant that sets out to create an experience. The décor is bright and evocative, with adobe walls and stepped friezes, the staff cheerful and the crowd young and artistically inclined. Dishes are traditional Arab and include chicken cooked in rosewater and vegetables in yoghurt sauce with rice, but the all-encompassing taster platter is probably the best option. Don't forget to have a look in Suite, south on Carrer Verdi (nos 3–5), for some designer wear on your way.

CATALAN THEATRE

8 Lliure de Gràcia

Carrer del Montseny, 47

The Lliure de Gràcia, located just north of the Plaça del Sol, is part of the Lliure theatre group, which has its own company of actors and directors, and includes a larger venue in Montjuïc (the Teatre Fabià Puigserver) with a separate, smaller theatre (the Espai Lliure) for experimental dance and theatre groups as well as lectures. The Gràcia venue presents a wide variety of productions in a modern space: plays by writers from Shakespeare to contemporary Catalan dramatists, readings by some of Catalunya's most prominent poets as well as concerts of classical music. There is a restaurant in the building, but with places like El Glop, Mesopotamia, Botafumeiro (p. 103) and Octubre (p. 104) nearby you might as well book a pre- or post-theatre table (though this may be tricky, as performances begin at 9:30 pm; on Sundays at 6:30).

A PLACE IN THE SUN

9 Plaça del Sol

This is an open, paved square surrounded by narrow 19th-century buildings, some of which have attractive Modernista designs painted pink, green and white with floral and geometric motifs (*esgrafiats*), swags and other adornments. In the 1980s architects Jaume Bach and Gabriel Mora redesigned the square, placing the parking below rather than above ground and adding trees, benches and shelter. During the day its merits are not immediately apparent, but in the evenings and on sunny days when the café tables come out and people gather to sit and drink or, later in the evening, meet up on their way to nearby club venues, the Plaça hums with life and feels very far away from the stifling touristic aspect of the Ramblas. Of the several surrounding bars, Café del Sol appears to be a classic haunt at first sight before you notice the groovier elements, the younger crowd and the piano in the back. Its narrow front bar area and back room fill up quickly as do the outdoor tables in nice weather.

MOORISH TEA ROOM

10 Tetería Jazmín

Carrer de Maspons, 11

This is an area known for its ethnic flavour and the Jazmín Tetería (one of Barcelona's unique tearoom-bars, see also Salterio, p. 22) is one of the more interesting stops. The brightly painted Moorish-style bar, complete with rounded arches, small intimate sitting areas and colourful mosaic decoration serves a selection of exotic teas, as well as cocktails, from 6 pm until 2 am.

DISCREETLY GOOD DINING

11 Roig Robi

TRIM AND TAILORED

12 Lydia Delgado

Gambas
Ostras
Almeja Viva
Vieira

GAUDÍ'S FIRST

13 Casa Vicens

Carrer de les Carolines, 24

You won't get inside this private residence, but no matter, the exterior will take your breath away. This, Antoni Gaudí's first major building commission and a triumph of the Modernista movement, is a visual cacophony, but ordering a large and varied range of materials is something for which the architect would come to be particularly known. Showing obvious Mudéjar influences, the façade combines swirling ironwork with vegetal motifs and green and yellow floral tiles against red brickwork, protruding bays, stylized geometric Moorish arches, stonework and more tiles. The assortment of ceramic tiles was a tribute to the owner, tile-manufacturer Manuel Vicens Montaner, who must have surely been pleased with the result since it shows them off to such tremendously appealing effect. The house originally included large gardens with a mirador to overlook them. Although these have largely disappeared and despite the two later additions by other architects, the house still represents the early genius of one of the world's most innovative architects.

HILLSIDE SEAFOOD

14 Botafumeiro

Carrer Gran de Gràcia, 81

It's a remove from the ports of Barceloneta but large, luxurious Botafumeiro casts a gaze oceanwards with a clear nautical theme and seafood-based menu showing its Galician heritage. You'll find men in suits smoking cigars, couples and groups sipping champagne and almost everyone enjoying oysters, shrimp, clams, squid and mussels by the platterful, not to mention the fresh baked sea bass, sole in butter with tiny shrimp and grilled hake. This is a well-established, formal and pricey establishment that has seen the likes of former President Clinton, the King of Spain and Julio Iglesias at its tables. Waiters are dressed in crisp white uniforms with brass buttons and epaulets signalling the maritime connection, while chef Moncho Neira, who founded the restaurant in the 1970s, leads the team of 'artists' in the kitchen.

INTERIOR WITH LINGERIE

15 De Lis

Carrer del Comte de Salvatierra, 10 bis

The mint green walls and dark modern woodwork would suit a trendy new bar or restaurant, but these tasteful interiors are home to the distinctive lingerie by Lis Beltran, a Barcelona designer who, after 10 years working for larger companies, decided to launch her own line of distinctive *ropa interior* in 1998. This is her first shop and the simple designs in deep colours (reflected in the shop's design) are meant, she says, 'for modern, intelligent women who aren't interested in anything too frilly but who nevertheless like a sense of mystery'. Lis's streamlined curves and vivid hues are a move away from 'traditional styles' to something more practical but also a lot more interesting for women who like to dress 'for themselves'.

IN ANY SEASON

16 Octubre

Carrer Julián Romea, 18

Even if the food, a mixture of Catalan and French, weren't wonderfully well prepared and reasonably priced the rustic chic intimacy, glimpsed through the paned windows, of stonework and brick offset with tidy tables, nice lighting and modern little decorative touches would draw you in. Octubre fits right in to the villagey atmosphere of Gràcia, where small, intimate spaces predominate and are full of surprises like this little gem of a dining room.

GARDEN OF THE 1970S SURREAL

17 Giardinetto

Carrer de la Granada del Penedès, 22

It's been here since 1974, when its arboretum-inspired interior won designers Frederico Correa and Alfonso Milà (see Plaça Reial, p. 30, and Flash Flash) an important design award with walls covered in dark green felt and scalloped along the top, where a leaf motif mirror resembles an overhanging tree. The bar is tucked away on the ground floor under a low ceiling and marked by a another tree made of mirrors. As the name suggests, it is Italian rather than Catalan cooking that the Giardinetto produces, with lots of home-made pastas. There is also a curious *ensalada al Algonquin Hotel Nueva York* on the menu, as well as more traditional seasonal specialties, and good basics like herb-encrusted beef. For all its throwback appeal, it's not cheap and you probably do need a reservation unless you just wander into the bar for a gimlet or something else suitably green.

OMELETTES FOR SWINGERS

18 Tortillería Flash-Flash

Carrer de la Granada del Penedès, 25

This is a case where cutting-edge has become classic or at least a must-see for all it holds of the evolution of Barcelona design. Frederico Correa and Alfonso Milà, who went on to weirder things with Giardinetto, designed this paean to photography and fashion in 1970, so the white-padded booths and bar and black-and-white photos of model Karin Leiz in numerous photographer poses are the real thing, though they could easily be mistaken for hip new retro. The place still attracts a crowd of high-brow artistic intelligentsia and high-heeled mannequin types for 100 different Spanish-style omelettes (*tortillas*) and other specialties.

CHAPEL OF THE BAROQUE

19 Capella de la Merced

Carrer de Laforja, 17

Built in 1795, this little church is now tightly squeezed between buildings on a narrow street. The interior is a surprising little burst of Baroque with marble facings, fluted pilasters and columns and vividly painted carved figures. For those interested in period architecture, the contrast with the sober solidity of the Gothic style of the Old City is remarkable.

BARCELONA CABARET

20 Luz de Gas

Carrer de Muntaner, 246

Having retained some of its turn-of-the-century period décor and charm, this former theatre has found a new lease of life hosting an array of live music, comedy, poetry and theatre performances. The entertainment changes every day, so it's best to phone ahead if you're in the mood for something special, otherwise just go along after drinks or dinner at the Giardinetto or Roig Robi (shows generally start at 11:30 pm). Despite its commodious interior it does get crowded, so be prepared to get close to someone.

ANNO D, 1795
RESTAURANT

INDUSTRIAL AVANT-GARDE

21 Otto Zutz

Carrer de Lincoln, 15

To experience the late nights for which Barcelona is famous, spend some of the wee hours at Otto Zutz. In a city as dynamic about design and club culture as Barcelona, it is saying something that Otto Zutz has managed to stay trendy, or at least very popular, for nearly two decades. Opened in 1985, this was high-style clubbing, with three dance floors and gallery spaces interspersed with chain-link fencing and giant photomurals that added to the industrial touches of the former textile factory. It still draws crowds of fashion fanatics and poseurs along with those dressed to kill, some in little more than beaded underwear, who fill the two large dance floors under the direction of a roster of international DJs.

LEADING EDGE

22 El Raco d'en Freixa

145

SCULPTURE AND JEWELS

23 Raimon Ollé

Carrer de Santaló, 39-41

From the look of the shop space you'd think Barcelona-born Raimon Ollé didn't believe in ornament; glass cases and bare walls make a stark background for his own creations. These works include not only his intricate, modern jewelry designs but also his largely ceramic sculpture. Of course both media inform each other, so Ollé's designs have appealing cross-over quality. The minimal space and contemporary design belie the artist's nearly 60 years in the business.

TASTEFUL LUXURIES

24 Semon

Carrer de Ganduxer, 31
Carrer de Santa Fe de Nou Mèxic, 25 (Semon 9)

Semon started as a gourmet food shop in the 1960s and their particular brand of regional produce is still available in their range of shops, restaurants and bars in Barcelona, Madrid and Marbella. Their latest venue, Semon 9, is an updated version with a bright, modern interior, where wine, champagne and Cava can be sipped by the glass while platters of their legendary foodstuffs are sampled or purchases mulled over. The shop at Ganduxer has a dining room open from 1pm, while Semon 9 opens at 9:30 am and also serves coffee.

SMOOTH OPERATOR

25 Tresserra Collection

Carrer de Josep Bertrand, 17

In his showroom, his serenely modern and minimal walnut furnishings and sculpture seem to float against a backdrop of white with stone floors quarried in Montjuïc, just as they do in some of the rooms he designed and furnished in Barcelona's towering Hotel Arts. Jaume Tresserra is Barcelona's premier furniture designer. His pieces have appeared in films from *Batman* and *A Kiss Before Dying* to *La Flor de Mi Secreto* to *Carne Tremulo* by Pedro Almodóvar, a director known for his scenic flair. Here in a stylish residential neighbourhood west of Gràcia, he presents a mere 40 pieces of his meticulously crafted collection. If the luxuriously smooth rich wood creations make your mouth water, head next door to L'Excellence du Sens du Vin for a quick *copa a la Francés* to wash down your order.

SUBURBAN SERENITY

26 Hotel Turó de Vilana

116

ABOVE THE FRAY

27 La Balsa

Carrer Infanta Isabel, 4

This wonderfully remote and secluded bower of a restaurant, on a steep hillside in a quiet residential street of Bonanova, was the creation of Oscar Tusquets and Lluis Clotet and won a prestigious design prize in 1979. The entrance is almost hidden in the vegetation, but a little gravel drive leads to an iron gate with an ant motif and next to it a small wall plaque bearing the name. Inside the courtyard, stairs lead up to the main restaurant level, a conservatory space filled with plants inside and an outdoor terrace also surrounded in greenery. The setting alone is worth a trip but the menu holds up as well. Described as 'international cuisine', the food is happily Spanish- and Catalan-based. Starters include *escudella de pagès* (peasant stew) and *crema de berros con huevo poche* (watercress soup with poached egg). *Croquetas des pescado y gambas con salsa estragón* (fish and shrimp croquettes in tarragon sauce), a stew of blood sausage (*morcilla*), chorizo and garbanzo beans or hake (*merluza*) in cuttlefish sauce are stars among the meat and fish dishes, which are joined by daily specials.

HEAD FOR THE HILLS

28 La Venta

LOST IN THE MUSIC

29 Walden 8

Avinguda de la Indústria, 12, Sant Just Desvern

Named in conjunction with Walden 7, an apartment building designed by architect Ricardo Bofill that looms in geometric asymmetry next door, and nothing to do with Henry David Thoreau as far as we know, Walden 8 is, in the late-20th-century trend, a dance club created from the hollowed space of a disused outlying factory building. However, this is much more than a few strobes and some iron catwalks. The design is an ambitious combination of a circular restaurant built around the old cement factory chimney, 100 feet (30 metres) up and overlooking the hilly landscape of Sant Just Desvern, just outside Barcelona. For an even better view you can climb the tower in a transparent glass lift to 300 feet (90 metres). Downstairs, the basement 'house floor' features ringed dance areas, chill-out spaces and 'cooler drinks' while the 'techno floor' pumps a faster beat in cavernous catacomb spaces that have all been given designer surreal touches. Dancing from midnight to 5 am. Restaurant opens 8:30 pm.

THE FAMILY VALUES

30 Gaig

Passeig de Maragall, 402

Carles Gaig may have inherited this top-notch restaurant, which, as the façade proudly notes, dates back to 1869, when it was opened by his great-grandparents, but his approach to Catalan and Mediterranean cuisine is far from antiquated. The building and interior have been updated recently to a thoroughly modern design, and the menu, though including some time-honoured recipes, is fresh and inventive. Gaig was awarded a Michelin star in 1993 and a national gastronomic prize in 2000. A choice of a gastronomic or à la carte menu includes starters like *bunyols de baccalà*, the ubiquitous salt cod, but this time in a light, puffy croquette, and various mains like baked pigeon or fresh fish, all followed by traditionally indulgent desserts such as hot (pudding-style) chocolate with stewed nectarines and yoghurt. Gaig is as serious about wine as he is about food, so an appropriate bottle is always available.

RUSTIC DESTINATION

31 Can Travi Nou

136

TRESSERRA
COLLECTION
RESTAURANT
DES DE 1869
RESTAURANTE La Balsa
Abierto de Lunes noche a Sábado noche.
De 14.00 a 15.30 y de 21.00 a 23.30 h.
Teléfono: 93 211 50 48

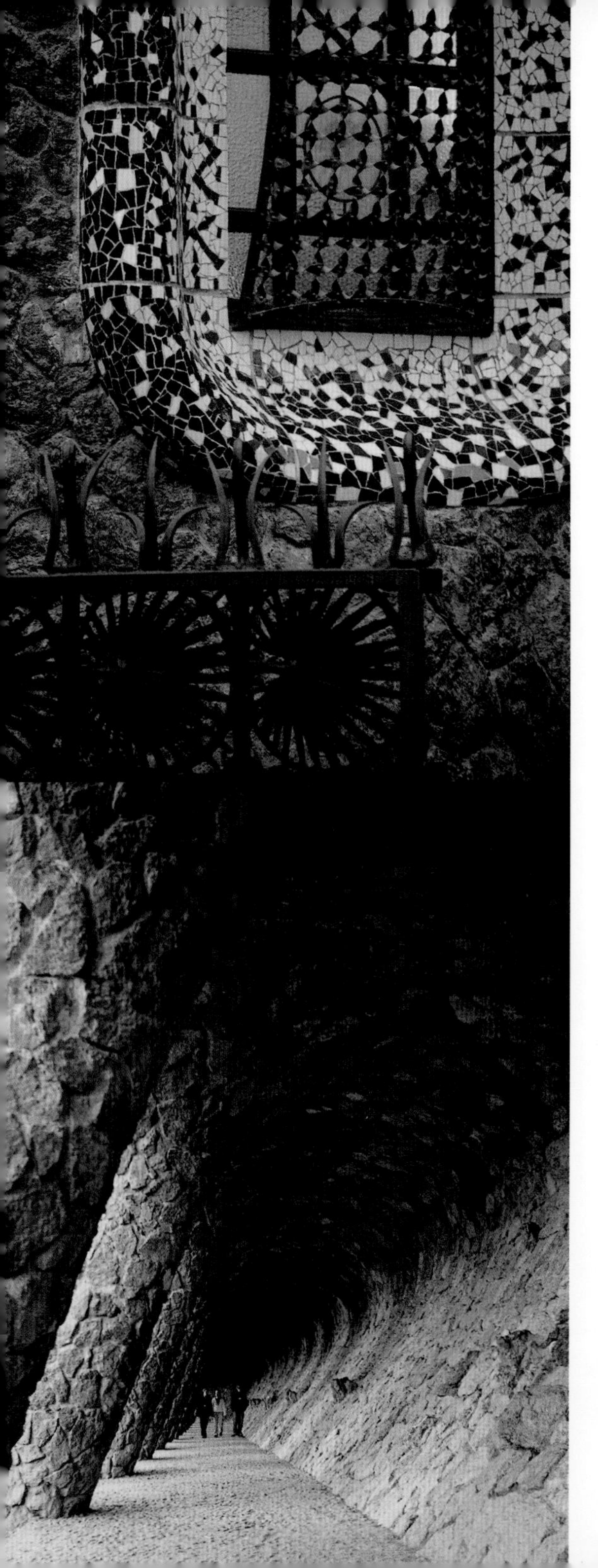

GAUDÍ IN WONDERLAND

32 Parc Güell

Carrer d'Olot

Declared a UNESCO world heritage site in 1984, the Park Güell (1900–14) was, after the Sagrada Familia, Antoni Gaudí's most ambitious project. It remains the largest in terms of area, covering a 50-acre (20-hectare) site and encompassing gatehouses, fountains, arcaded and elevated walkways, planters and viewing terraces. The grandest feature is the neoclassical hypostyle hall, which is at the top of a grand staircase watched over by a giant colourful salamander. Gaudí intended the hall for use as a shelter for local market stall-holders. Everywhere the curving, sculpted surfaces are clad in vibrant mosaics made from ceramic pieces called *trencadís* (or 'jigsaw pieces') and emblems and symbols from Catalan history are woven colourfully throughout. Gaudí's patron, Eusebi Güell (see Palau Güell, p. 63) had envisioned the park as an English-style, green space that would be used by the residents of a new, elite housing development he planned to build. Part of the enduring appeal lies in the fact that the architect insisted on working with the existing, undulating landscape, so the elements rise up on hillsides and are overlooked at different levels. The houses were never built, but the park in all its elite idealism remains a wondrous product of creative genius given free, subsidized rein.

MONASTERY GALLERY

33 Monestir de Pedralbes Thyssen Bornemisza Collection

Baixada de Monestir, 9

The Order of St Clare was established here, in what is today a well-heeled suburb of La Serra, in the 14th century on the site of the *petras albas*, or white rocks, by Queen Elisenda de Montcada, wife of King Jaume II. The church and cloister are built in the Catalan Gothic style, the cloister rising delicately three storeys, and much of the medieval structure survives. The 14th-century frescoes in the Chapel of Sant Miquel, for example, are still extraordinarily vivid. The main hall of the palace attached to the monastery and some of the dormitory rooms are now a luminous backdrop for the Thyssen Bornemisza Collection of Pedralbes. Paintings and sculpture from the medieval period, Germanic and Italian Renaissance, European Baroque and Late Venetian Baroque include works by Fra Angélico, Lucas Cranach, Lorenzo Lotto, Titian, Tintoretto, Rubens, Tiepolo and Canaletto, as well as altar-pieces, religious portraits and sculpture.

Style Traveller

sleep

Although the trend for highly sophisticated boutique-style hotels has not caught on with great force in this most design-conscious of cities, there are waves of change set to roll. At present, a range of accommodation from cutting-edge bargain to old-world elegance and from mid-century modern classic to new designer lodgings are available and the best of these rival any of the biggest and best in much larger cities. All of those featured here offer something particular to themselves and to Barcelona that make them worth choosing from among the rest. And most are a stone's throw from some of the most enchanting urban sights to be visited in Europe.

SUBURBAN SERENITY

96 Hotel Turó de Vilana

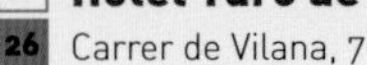

26 Carrer de Vilana, 7

Double rooms from €175

Bonanova is actually not that far away from the centre of Barcelona, especially by city train, but it is worlds away from the busy streets of the old city or even the Eixample in terms of quiet and calm. Perhaps that is why the Barcelona family behind this operation decided on this spot in a largely residential area to build a small hotel (only 20 rooms) that is imbued with a certain relaxed elegance. Built in 1996, the structure itself capitalizes on natural light and the surrounding greenery, with clerestory windows and skylights in the public areas. Unlike other Barcelona hotels that rely on the cosy, antique charms of the Barri Gòtic, Raval and Ribera, or even the imposing, multistorey Modernista masterworks of the Eixample, the Turó de Vilana takes full advantage of the opportunity to be modern and spacious, light and airy. The interiors have been done to a high standard with honey-coloured wood and light marble in clean-lined spaces. Anything remotely dark or cramped seems to have been banished from the premises.

The rooms on all three floors are soundproofed, with marble bathrooms, full air conditioning and double-glazing, so even if there were noise on the street, chances are you wouldn't hear it. Five of the rooms have terraces, which afford a nice view from this hillside setting. There is a restaurant that serves a breakfast buffet. As for dinner, guests are enviously close to La Balsa (see p. 108) though it is advisable to take a cab, as it is a fairly steep walk uphill. From the hotel it is about a 10-minute walk to either the Tibidabo or Sarrià train station, which has service similar to the metro (and at the same price) where the trains go directly (about another 10 minutes) to Plaça de Catalunya with stops along the way. Otherwise the helpful staff can advise you on bus and taxi services. The monastery of Pedralbes (see p. 111) and the Parc Güell (see p. 111) are both within easy reach of the hotel by taxi.

OLD SPANISH STYLE

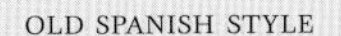

60 Hotel Mesón Castilla

25 Carrer de Valldonzella, 5
Double rooms from €130

A rare glimpse of Spanish Colonial style in Barcelona, the Mesón Castilla mixes Old World charm with modern convenience in a location just a stone's throw from the hub of Plaça de Catalunya. Opened in 1952, the hotel is a quiet world unto itself. There are 57 rooms arranged on five floors but the spaces on the first floor, part of the original, smaller hotel, are undoubtedly the most characterful, with heavy furniture and woodwork painted with floral motifs. There are quiet sitting rooms on each floor, with sofas, armchairs and newspapers available. The sitting room on the first floor is, again, more elaborate, with murals and red and green painted woodwork. Here there is also a larger public room with sitting areas and television just outside the rather grand, wood-panelled breakfast room where the generous buffet breakfasts are served and which also has an outdoor terrace. The upper rooms are more spare but with some nice decorative touches and antiques, and all are immaculate and well-presented. Some rooms have balconies and there are some larger, family-style rooms available. All the rooms have television, air-conditioning and mini-bars (there is also underground parking). Many have a view, which is only of the streets below, but it is worth requesting, as these are generally brighter and airier than those without. The catering is breakfast only but there are restaurants and tapas bars aplenty in this neighbourhood bordering the Raval and the Barri Gòtic

The overall atmosphere is of understated elegance. Service is smooth, facilities have been modernized and the style has been updated without being overwrought. Even with the Ramblas, the Plaça de Catalunya, the University and MACBA (see p. 71) close by, the hotel manages to maintain a calm, steady service that makes for a relaxing base to which to return.

FASHIONABLE NEW FAVOURITE

42 **Hotel Banys Orientals**

2 Carrer de l'Argenteria, 37
Double rooms from €100

This is a place you look at and think, 'someone somewhere had a great idea'. Though this is one of Barcelona's newest hotels, it would be difficult to find one better placed for exploring the streets of the old city or with more stylish, modern facilities. Just around the corner from the historic Carrer de Montcada (see p. 50) and just metres from the magical Santa Maria del Mar, the Hotel Banys Orientals is one of Barcelona's most design-conscious hotels but at the same time it manages to maintain some of the most reasonable tariffs. This is the centre of the Ribera between the cultural counterpoints of the Barri Gòtic and the hugely lively Passeig del Born. This kind of hotel would be a treat in any city, but in such a boutique of a city, it really does put you in the heart of things.

The public areas and 44 rooms are all decorated in sleek, minimal style but with the warmth of dark wood, a few antiques, artworks set here and there and some notable design objects, including contemporary four-poster beds and lucite chairs by Philippe Starck, set discreetly around. These are offset by white gauzy curtains and crisp white bedlinen. There are no suites, but eleven rooms have small balconies overlooking the narrow medieval streets. The stunning modern character reflects the confluence of art and design in the nearby recently gentrified Born area, but it is much more than a superficial makeover; this is a hotel on a par with some of the trendier accommodation in New York and London.

Started by a group of private investors, one of whom is the owner of the classic Senyor Parellada restaurant downstairs, the Banys Orientals opened in May of 2002, in a happy juxtaposition of tasteful new enterprise and respect for the historic building. The special relationship with the Senyor Parellada means that you can enter the restaurant through the hotel lobby and the hotel breakfast is served there. Also, being a guest will help you get your reservations at the revered dining spot. Such an updated sense of design in such a prime location packed with some of the best eating, drinking, sightseeing and shopping Barcelona has to offer sounds too good to be true but, luckily for us, now it isn't.

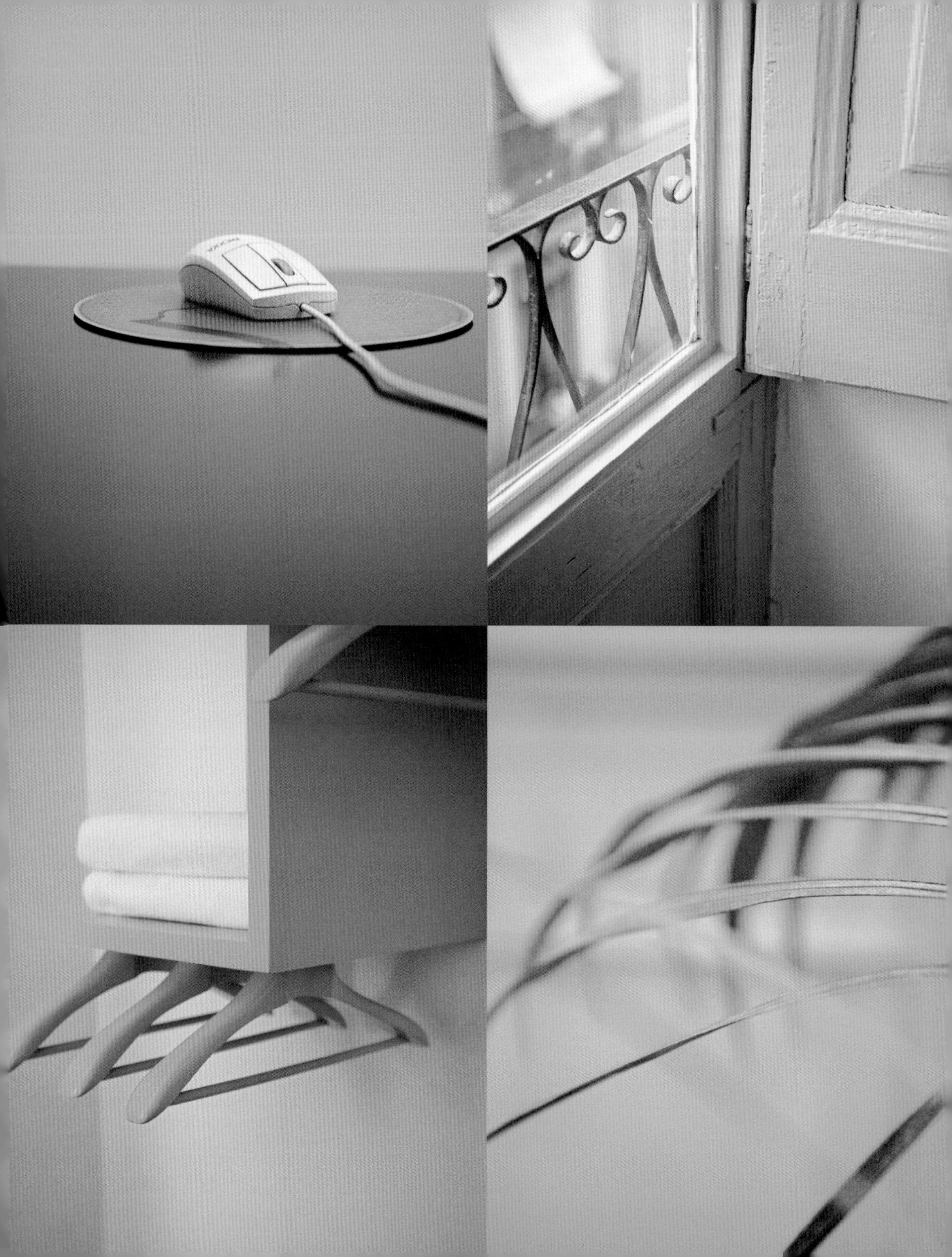

BRIGHT YOUNG THING

60 Hostal Gat Raval

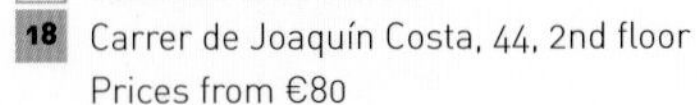

18 Carrer de Joaquín Costa, 44, 2nd floor
Prices from €80

When the children of a hotelier family based in Madrid wanted to start an enterprise of their own, it was no surprise that they chose the hospitality industry. But for people brought up on luxury accommodation the Hostal Gat Raval is something of a departure. It speaks of their youthful ingenuity that they realized a gap in the market for good simple service that would attract young travellers and members of the more experienced set who were more concerned with good value than frills. So the Gat Raval was born, fusing a bright, high-tech look with basic accommodation. The location, too, is appropriate, in the heart of the Raval, not far from the artistic buzz around MACBA (p. 71) on a street whose formerly less inviting establishments are being redesigned and refurbished to bring in new, trendy spots. 'Cool and clean' is their mantra, and that is the overall feeling.

The rooms have different layouts and views (it's worth bearing in mind that of the 24 rooms, only eight have private baths), some of which take in the MACBA and some overlook an inner courtyard. Against the profusion of light and air, green and black elements fill every room, and each features a lighted photographic scene of the Raval area. Guests have to go out for food, but with the Rambla and La Boqueria (see p. 67) so close by, as well as the profusion of ethnic and designer restaurants in the area, finding something good to eat is more a question of choosing between options than of finding something suitable.

MODERNISTA STYLE

80

Hotel Condes de Barcelona

23 Passeig de Gràcia, 73–75

Double rooms from €240

Occupying the Casa J. Daurella (1872) and the Casa Enric Battló (1895; not to be confused with Gaudí's Casa Battló at no. 43) across two corners of the Carrer de Mallorca, the Condes de Barcelona is an education in Modernista architecture, at least on the outside. This area, known as the Quadrat d'Or, is well-populated with Modernista buildings, and on the luxury-lined Passeig de Gràcia even the pavement sports Art Nouveau motifs. So if you're a Modernista buff then you might want to plant yourself here or, better yet, on the hotel roof terrace, where you can have an uninterrupted, almost eye-level view of the fantastical roof decoration of Gaudí's Casa Milà (La Pedrera).

Both buildings that make up the Condes de Barcelona – Casa Daurella is no. 73, Casa Battló no. 75 – were enlarged and renovated in 1997, and the interiors have been completely remodelled in a thoroughly contemporary style by Josep Juanpere and Antoni Puig. The dramatic architecture of Modernista buildings on the Passeig de Gràcia is a hard act to follow, so it is no wonder that the designers opted for nice touches of colour and texture, including the use of plush 'Modernista green' fabrics, wood floors and artistic flourishes that allude to rather than try to emulate the style and period of the architecture. This is a full-service luxury hotel and offers all the conveniences that that implies, with a few extras. Rooms overlooking the Passeig de Gràcia are of course in demand, but there are others, in no. 75, that overlook a skylit interior courtyard. And guests in both buildings have use of the roof terrace and swimming pool at no. 75, which offers a truly remarkable experience and a privileged vantage point from which to survey the Eixample. While no. 75 does have the rooftop amenities, the Thalassa restaurant and a comfortably formal bar, as well as some surviving elements of period decoration, the other building is no grudging compromise. The décor and room service are of an equally high standard, and details such as the lobby skylight and bold works of art make a thematic link with the other building. No. 73 also has the distinction of being markedly quieter.

REBIRTH OF THE COOL

42 **Park Hotel**

30 Avinguda Marquès de l'Argentera, 11

Double rooms from €150

Opened in 1957, the Park Hotel is a small mid-century landmark straddling the boundary between the Ribera and Barceloneta. With the port just a short walk away, it exhibits the air of a seaside hotel, especially as the ground-floor bar has a window that can be opened up to serve outside. The glass block and turquoise tile on the curving corner façade sound the first note of 1950s modern, but there is plenty more to follow, including the squared spiral stair, perforated balcony partitions and the wonderfully retro bar itself.

The hotel was originally designed by architect Antoni Moragas i Gallisa, who was influenced by Alvar Aalto and Gio Ponti, among others, and it was something of a design statement in its heyday. Like many Barcelona gems it had a period of neglect but it has been undergoing steady refurbishment since 1990, when it had its first overall makeover. Then, in 2001, the management embarked on a concentrated scheme to renovate one floor every year. With only seven floors and a total of 91 rooms that suggests a great attention to detail. The enlarged period photographs of the building in the lobby walls demonstrate the owner's dedication to recapturing some of the former glory, and it's not hard to imagine how cool it must have once been. While some elements might lack the polish they once had, the design is so genuine and of-a-piece that it scarcely matters. Add to this the proximity to the celebrated new restaurant Abac (see p. 132) downstairs. The restaurant serves as the hotel breakfast buffet until noon, which means you start the day in fine surroundings. Afterwards the formal restaurant takes over, so you should book a table if you intend to have dinner or lunch there.

The rooms retain their 1950s design elements but have been updated with dark brown suede-style fabrics, dark wood and white linen. Rooms with terraces overlook the boulevard and the large Plaça del Palau. Guests here are well-placed for exploring Barceloneta and sampling fantastic tapas and seafood, from the high-end delights of Passadis del Pep (p. 130) and high-flying tapas of La Estrella de Plata (p. 141) to the more traditional Can Solé (p. 57) and 7 Portes (p. 57).

eat

Barcelona is no longer just the land of cheap seafood, *pa amb tomàquet* (bread rubbed with tomato, olive oil and salt) and tapas bars. Though Catalan staple foods have not by any means been diluted into something blandly familiar, the gastronomic experience of Barcelona is as varied as in any cosmopolitan city. Yes, there are the comfortable and casual *platillos* and tapas, but there are also tapas elevated to an art form. Recently, fusion cuisine has swept through kitchens both *haute* and trendy, in which traditional Catalan ingredients take on the touches of international cooking. Don't expect a sit-down lunch before 2 pm or dinner before 8 pm – but do expect to be thrilled.

THE CHEF KNOWS BEST

42 Passadís del Pep

32 Plaça del Palau, 2

Down an anonymous passage off the Plaça del Palau is one of those places that intimidate tourists with their own peculiar way of doing things, namely that they don't hand out menus but start serving up portions of wonderful fare along with glasses of Cava almost as soon as someone takes a seat. The bright figures painted on the walls are just visible at the end of the entrance corridor and signal the upbeat atmosphere of this popular and prestigious restaurant run by Pep Manubens whose Cal Pep (Plaça de Olles, 8) is a less expensive tapas version. Diners are offered Cava along with a preliminary *pica-pica* plate of ham, mussels and oysters and then a fish or seafood course that depends upon what's fresh that day. A pricey but incomparable way to sample Barcelona dining.

FINE OLD-FASHIONED

60 Casa Leopoldo

30 Carrer Sant Rafael, 24

A family-run restaurant that has been attracting artists and intellectuals since 1929, Casa Leopoldo is full of old-fashioned Spanish charm, from the authentic *azulejos* (Spanish decorative tiles) and wood furniture to the bullfighting photos on the walls. This is not one of the Raval's trendy new additions but a legendary favourite. The menu is robust Catalan fare, with lots of grilled fish and shellfish, stewed tripe and beef and home-made pastries. A particularly interesting specialty of scrambled eggs with prawns and garlic seems to be on everyone's top ten. The homey atmosphere belies a serious approach to traditional cuisine, to which the bill will attest.

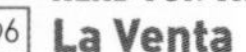

96 La Venta

28 Plaça del Doctor Andreu

Sitting prettily on the hillside next to the terminus of Barcelona's last remaining tramline, La Venta is neither the anachronism nor the tourist haunt you might expect. Quaint boxes of flowers and well-tended shrubs surrounding the conservatory-like space and outdoor terrace make a picturesque setting for the high-quality Spanish cuisine that keeps La Venta popular with a well-dressed clientele who come en masse in families and groups on weekends and in steady flow most weekdays. The menu is varied, including standbys like *butifarra* (Catalan sausage), fried squid, grilled monkfish (*rape*), hake (*merluza*) and other fish, as well as the less traditional *lasaña de salmón ahumado* (lasagne with smoked salmon) and hearty game and beef, all prepared to a high standard.Take the Tramvia Blau from Plaça John F. Kennedy; from here you might want to continue uphill on the funicular to take in the view of the city from Tibidabo before returning for a memorable lunch or dinner.

MODERN CLASSIC

42 Abac

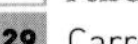

29 Carrer del Rec, 79–89

Xavier Pellicer, one of the bright young talents of Catalan cooking, was awarded a Michelin star for his restaurant in 1999 and continues to turn out a menu of original dishes inspired by but not confined to his native country. The background too has been orchestrated to enhance the enjoyment of the cuisine. Every detail of the restaurant's discreet, modern décor has been chosen carefully to coincide with the immaculate presentation of food: Pellicer even commissioned a sculptor to create a 'tower' for the petit fours. Bamboo-steamed foie gras and crab tartare show Pellicer's affinity for fusion cuisine, as do tuna topped with squid, broccoli and mango and the fennel and shrimp ravioli. There is also a tasting menu that is sure to evoke plenty of oohs and ahhhs.Though they serve the breakfast buffet for guests of the Park Hotel in the mornings (see p. 126), in the afternoon and evenings these are some of Barcelona's most coveted tables.

80 Principal (El Principal del Tragaluz)

28 Carrer de Provença, 286–88

The feather in the cap of the Grupo Tragaluz (see Tragaluz, p. 90), which has recently branched into the hotel business with OMM (opening in autumn 2003 on the corner of Roselló and Passeig de Gràcia), Principal is everything a high-end formal restaurant should be with the added flair of Barcelona design and style. The interior in this transformed Eixample townhouse is unhesitatingly sleek and elegant, from the dark wood tables and designer lighting to the tall, uncovered windows overlooking Carrer Provença. Movable panels allow staff to give groups from eight to 220 private space. Despite the chain-like connotations of Grupo Tragaluz, the menu is inventive and successful: lobster broth with garlic and basil; veal carpaccio with *mousse de ceps*; steamed hake with creamed rice, sundried tomato, onion and pimento; monkfish with a crispy sliver of fried artichoke and romesco sauce (tomato, oil, red pepper and crushed almonds). Their taste for Japanese cooking (evident in their restaurant Japonés) appears in tempura vegetable and seafood selections.

MY DINNER WITH GAUDÍ

80 **Casa Calvet**

4 Carrer de Casp, 48

It has the distinction of being set within a prime piece of Modernista architecture, Gaudí's first building in the Eixample. So the restaurant doesn't need to try too hard to draw customers. However, along with the delightful exterior and interior decoration that is a visual feast of tiles, stained glass and carved woodwork, the Casa Calvet offers an excellent menu of Catalan cuisine. There is also a *dégustacion* (tasting) menu that might include duck foie gras, artichokes on a bed of baked onion with almond creme, monkfish in herbed oil, venison in juniper 'perfume' with redcurrant sauce and a selection of equally intriguing desserts. The wine list and service are similarly high-class. A rare opportunity to experience two of the finer points of Catalan culture.

GOURMET LESSONS

42 **Hofmann**

9 Carrer de l'Argentería, 74–78

A bright contemporary façade near Santa Maria del Mar signals the location of Mey Hofmann's restaurant and cooking school. You might also notice the students standing outside in their kitchen whites having a break. Upstairs in the unostentatious and quite homely surroundings Hofmann produces her own brand of high Catalan cuisine. There is also a pleasant, plant-lined courtyard patio. Hofmann admits that she likes to indulge in fantasy, to present dishes that 'seduce, provoke and tempt' diners towards something that will leave 'the most stimulating sensations on the palate'. This she accomplishes with seemingly tame concoctions like sautéed lobster with chick peas and tender onion, sea bream with bacon and red wine, and lamb with mustard on a bed of aubergines, tomato and squash. The menu changes regularly but is limited to a few exquisitely prepared courses. Desserts, too, are a lesson in perfection.

HIGH ROMANCE

80 **Drolma**

19 Passeig de Gràcia, 68

One of Barcelona's most desirable dining locations is a secluded little group of tables up a red-carpeted marble staircase in the luxurious Hotel Majestic. Vintage photographs line the stair but this interior is all new, opened in 1999, and eschews contemporary minimalism for a taste of the romantic, Art Nouveau past. The maître d' in morning dress will escort you past the velvet draperies to the narrow room of tables that overlook the Passeig de Gràcia and Carrer de València. Chef Fermí Puig follows the current Barcelona trend for tasting menus made up of a series of gastronomic fantasies, such as pheasant cannelloni in foie gras sauce with black truffles, or giant prawns with wild mushrooms. Puig also excels at classics with his own twist, such as scallops (*vieiras*) and asparagus; *congrio* (eel) with potatoes; whole, acorn-fed duck for two; or beef with cherry and apricot chutney. Desserts range from rich chocolate and rhubarb soufflé to caramelized pineapple with rosewater and cinnamon sorbet.

RUSTIC DESTINATION

 **Can Travi Nou**

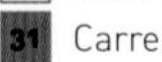 Carrer Jorge Manrique

This is a taxi destination, but worth the expense for traditional Catalan fare and atmosphere. The building dates from the early 18th century when it lay on the old road of Sant Cebrià but was renovated in the 1920s and turned into something like a country manor. Massive wood beams and a large stone hearth dominate the interior, while vine-covered walls and a lushly planted terrace make for a picturesque exterior, both signalling the pleasant country-style approach to food and service. Owners Josep Soler i Cuixart and Tere Ribatallada i Simó started up the restaurant in the 1980s with the idea of recreating a rural retreat in the middle of the city. Here they proudly present dishes like *sípia amb mandoguilles* (squid with meatballs) and *bolets al forn amb all i pernil* (baked wild mushrooms, garlic and ham), *xai al forn amb patates, ceba i tomàquets* (lamb with potatoes, onion and tomato) and home-made pastries to top it all off.

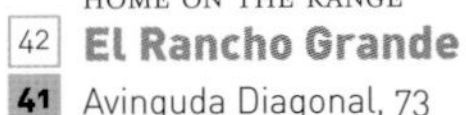

HOME ON THE RANGE

42 **El Rancho Grande**

41 Avinguda Diagonal, 73

The thrill is in finding it. The building is unmarked, except for the address (you'll need a taxi to get there). Catalunya's top new cutting-edge and most modern designers have not laid a finger on this place (though many frequent it). And neither have the city planners, as it couldn't be in a less salubrious urban setting where roads are broken and the great Diagonal almost comes to an end at the water's edge. But this is probably all to the good for Rancho Grande, a home-style restaurant that looks like a converted garage and has earned its place in the hearts of many Barcelonans who venture here for the honest, no-frills cooking personally prepared by the Mallorcan husband and wife who own the place. There is no menu, only platters of cold meat sitting on every table and the sound of the fresh-caught fish and meat sizzling away on a massive grill (*brasa*). If language is a problem, you'll be escorted to a case of fresh fish and asked to point. When your food arrives, you can be sure it will be fresh and hearty – a genuine celebration of life's good things.

SWEET SURRENDER

42 **Espai Sucre**

26 Carrer de la Princesa, 53

The lighted orange sign with the black ant signals one of Barcelona's most unusual restaurants. Pastry chef Jordi Butrón opened this paean to *postres*, which is a school for pastry chefs during the day and a restaurant devoted to sweets at night. The interior is attractive, with a very modern, sophisticated design by Alfons Tost (see also Comerç 24, next page). The kitchen does serve some savoury dishes but only as a prelude to the all-important dessert courses. So salads such as couscous with ginger and pumpkin or lentil and foie gras soup are followed by El Gran Menu de Postres or El Pequeño (consisting of three or five courses). This might mean a soup of a different kind, featuring lychees with apple, celery and almonds, or a strawberry sponge (*bizcocho*) that's not nearly as plain or simple as it sounds.

INDUSTRIAL FUSION

42 **Comerç 24**

24 Carrer del Comerç, 24

One of the bold new design statements in the Born, Comerç 24 takes its cooking seriously too. The grey-green walls with red-upholstered corners and plush pillows and cymbal chandeliers are part of a seriously design-led atmosphere created by Alfons Tost (compare the squared shapes of Espai Sucre, previous page), Xavier Abellán and Anna Rius. Meanwhile, chef Carlos Abellán produces a 'festival' menu that rivals some of the most innovative cooking in Catalonia today, which is saying something. Some still call it tapas, but superstar chef Ferran Adrià (of El Bulli, see p. 180) has elevated small courses to grander heights, and Abellán has made his own contribution to the trend with dishes like asparagus in whipped grapefruit purée, sausage-stuffed squid and some Japanese-Italian-American fusions. Desserts mix sweet and savoury in a nod to the latest revival of traditional Catalan favourites that seems to be sweeping through the newest Barcelona kitchens.

BRIGHT YOUNG STAR

42 **Santa Maria**

28 Carrer del Comerç, 17

'Designer tapas' is how some people describe the cuisine of young, photogenic and much-publicized chef Paco Guzmán. Having trained under Ferran Adrià (see El Bulli, p. 180), he has turned the culinary arts of one of Spain's most celebrated kitchens to exquisite little portions, literally exploding with flavour. His avant-garde concoctions include marinated sardines with aubergine and yoghurt, or carpaccio with spinach, artichokes and cheese. Finish off with a crackling Dracula (cola and raspberry) or Lola (passion-fruit) mousse.

STAR-QUALITY TAPAS

42 La Estrella de Plata

31 Plaça del Palau, 13

Chef Didac López and his team of young chefs produce gourmet-style tapas in a high-flying setting to match both the quality and the prices. This is one of Barcelona's most fashionable (and expensive) tapas bars. While others might be happily low-key and good quality, this place is pushing boundaries on all sides. In some ways it seems that nouvelle cuisine was just made for tapas, as each platter is a mini-course in art and gastronomy. With a good choice of wine and fine service it all adds up to a truly star-quality experience.

96 **Ot**

3 Carrer Torres, 25

Fish, seahorses and other marine life prance about in primary colours across the walls and dinnerware of this small, vibrant dining room where the décor is matched only by the gastronomic sensations. Ot made a splash when it first opened the doors in 1996 and they're still turning people away. This is not just because they have only eight tables and so room for a mere 24 people, but because chef Ferran Caparros's approach to Mediterranean fusion has made Ot one of Gràcia's best-loved dining spots. The changing menu might feature *sopa de tomate con gambas* (tomato soup with prawns), *llenguado con compota de albaricoque y espárragos con holandesa de vainilla* (sole with apricot compote and asparagus with vanilla hollandaise sauce) and a pudding of fresh fruit served with hot chocolate soup topped with cinnamon and granules of *horchata* (tiger-nut milk). Best to book ahead, early in the week for the weekend.

CUISINE ON HIGH

42 **Torre d'Alta Mar**

38 Passeig Joan de Borbó, 88

If you want to experience a really memorable view of the port and city, and you aren't afraid of heights, then take the 75-metre-high ride up to the Torre d'Alta Mar and discover one of Barcelona's most glamorous dining spots. Chef Óscar Manresa's Mediterranean menu is one of the priciest in town and the food, though pleasantly simple, is not always as exquisite as the vista (and given the restaurant's high-society profile, the scene inside can be almost as intriguing as the one through the window). But taken as a whole, the Torre d'Alta Mar amounts to a fine way to spend a lunchtime or evening. There are good standbys such as razor clams or sautéed squid and mushrooms, and sea cucumber and sea snails for starters. Mains are dominated by an assortment of fresh fish served baked or grilled.

DISCRETELY GOOD DINING

96 **Roig Robi**

11 Carrer de Séneca, 20

Small, quiet Carrer de Séneca looks at first like a street set for assignations of one sort or another until you notice the high-end design shops through the windows. The Roig Robi is no exception to the luxury trend here or the idea of assignations, since it is the picture of discretion, with the dining room set well back from the doorbelled entrance. It features smart, minimal wood interior, a green tile floor, artworks and a wide patio garden in back, and is family-run by Mercé Navarro (paintings are by family friend Antoni Tàpies). Truffles figure prominently on the seasonal menu, which boasts updated Catalan cooking by Mrs Navarro herself. They appear in a cheese souffle (*suflé de formatge i tòfona*) or in an onion and foie gras tart for starters or in a main of poulard stuffed with apple, goose liver and truffle. Rice with sea cucumbers and artichokes is both traditional and inventive. As opposed to some of the simple seafood presentations found elsewhere in Barcelona, fish here is dressed up with crispy leeks, porcini mushrooms or garlic sauce (*salsa melosa d'alls*).

THE NAME OF HAUTE CUISINE

96 **Jean Luc Figueras**

2 Carrer de Santa Teresa, 10

A chef known to have spawned a number of young Barcelona cooking talents, Jean Luc Figueras still maintains a hold on one of the city's top restaurants. Its location in the former studio and showroom of fashion designer Cristobal Balenciaga doesn't hurt, but the cuisine certainly stands up without the glamorous backdrop. Salad of scallops with lentils and *tocinillos* (a pudding made of egg yolk), salmon fillet with white truffle cream, cold rosemary and orange soup with black olive paste and walnuts are among the selection of traditional dishes with French overtones, which also includes an adventurous tasting menu and a selection of desserts made by the man himself and described by at least one satisfied diner as 'magisterial'.

LEADING EDGE

96 El Racó d'en Freixa

22 Carrer de Sant Elíes, 22

Talented young chef Ramón Freixa does classics and his own inventive dishes with determined style and grace and is becoming one of Barcelona's top chefs. The restaurant was opened in 1986 and Ramón Freixa took over the kitchen in 1997. By 2001 he was named the best Spanish chef by Spain's *Guia Gourmetour* among a string of accolades and starred placements including one at the Manoir aux Quatre Saisons, Oxford, achieved before the age of 30. The menu can be traditional or full of surprises: a starter of cocoa pastry filled with mushrooms, vegetables and chestnuts, with bacon ice-cream; a variety of fish baked in aromatic Thai broth; and, to finish, coconut cannelloni with caramel yoghurt, aniseed flan and coconut, corn and curry ice-cream. The décor is not quite as adventurous, but who's looking at the walls when there is so much art on the plate?

CUISINE OF KINGS

60 Ca l'Isidre

2 Carrer de Les Flors, 12

The blank, blond wood and frosted glass exterior do not hint that this place has been here for 32 years. The name is barely visible, neatly etched into the concrete to the left of the doorway. And when you push through the door you feel like you've entered someone's private hallway with photos and awards of the Gironés family. Down the narrow hall, the glassed-in kitchen becomes visible, then you turn a corner to find a sophisticated dining room full of well-dressed waiters and clients and perhaps only then do you appreciate the refined dining experience that is about to commence. This is a family-run restaurant that has reached the top both in terms of quality and clientele, counting King Juan Carlos among their generations of satisfied customers. Elements of high society and design aside, the reason for their success is undoubtedly their consistently excellent dishes featuring fresh local produce, such as lamb, prepared to a high standard in very basic Catalan and Spanish traditional style. Specialties include marinated goat (*cabrit*).

drink

In the land where chocolate has its own guilds, associations and a new museum, the afternoon hot drink of choice among some people is often a thick cup of the stuff topped with a large lump of pure, fresh cream (*a suizo*), which can be had in the many old-fashioned milk bars (or *granjas*). Tea is making inroads in some exotic *teterias*, where varieties of infusions are served alongside cocktails. The latter are reaching new heights of popularity in a wave of boldly designed retro-future-high-tech bars and clubs, many concentrated around the Born. And then there are the Cava and wine bars, some elegant and cool, some funky, fitted into Gothic spaces, all extraordinarily atmospheric.

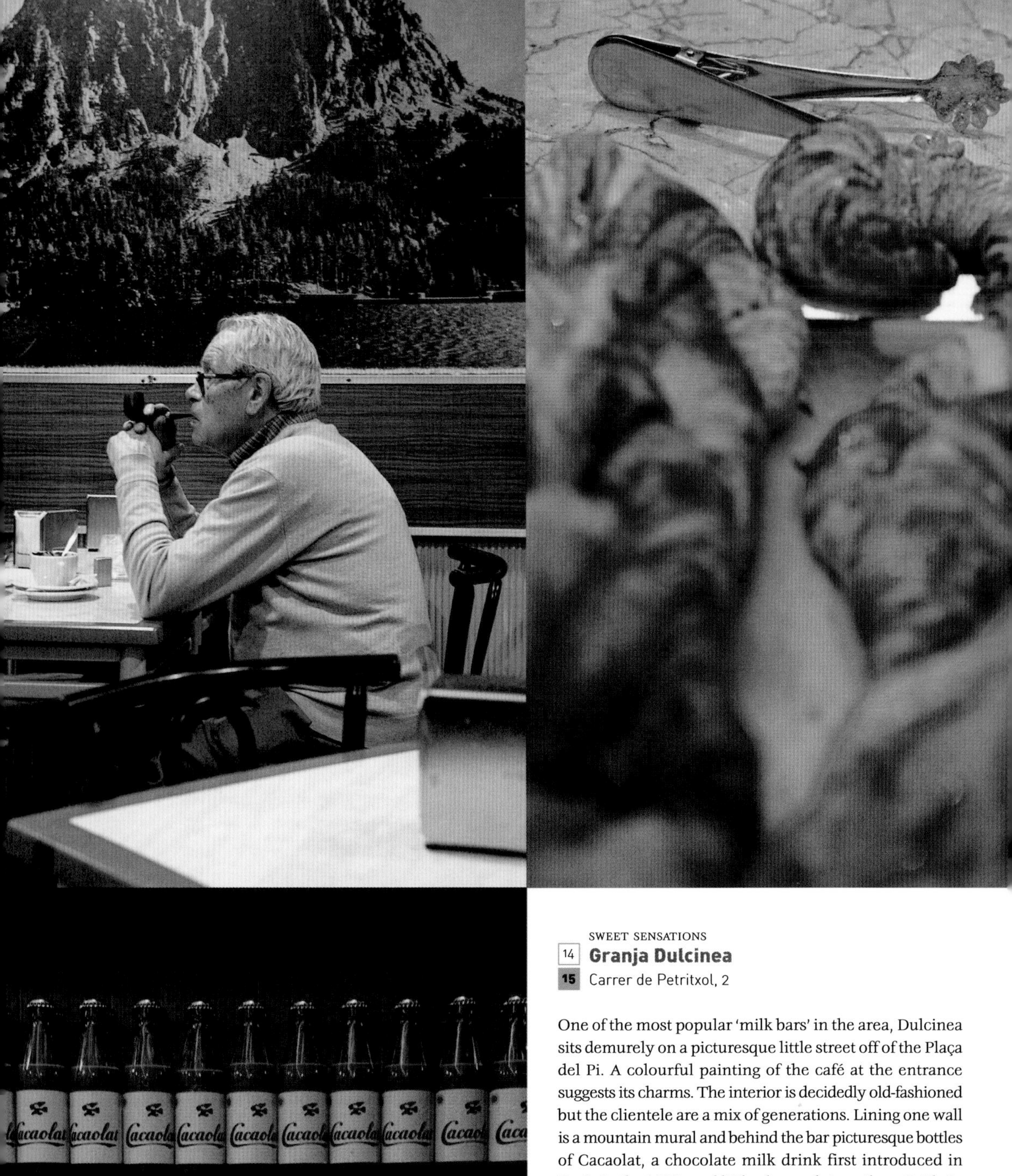

SWEET SENSATIONS

14 **Granja Dulcinea**

15 Carrer de Petritxol, 2

One of the most popular 'milk bars' in the area, Dulcinea sits demurely on a picturesque little street off of the Plaça del Pi. A colourful painting of the café at the entrance suggests its charms. The interior is decidedly old-fashioned but the clientele are a mix of generations. Lining one wall is a mountain mural and behind the bar picturesque bottles of Cacaolat, a chocolate milk drink first introduced in Spain in the 1930s and little changed since then. Settle in and combat the afternoon's low blood sugar in true Barcelona style with a thick hot chocolate and something sweet and doughy to go with it.

CAKES AND ART

60 **Escribà**

12 Rambla de les Flors, 83

People are drawn in first by the glittering Modernista façade with its violet and green mosaic, Art Nouveau stained glass and swirling decorative motifs. 'We don't only make cakes, we create illusions' is the motto of this pastry-making dynasty that has held Barcelona in a sugar-induced thrall since Mateu Serra i Capell started his bakery on the Gran Via in 1906. Today Christian Escribà presides over the family empire with a legendary reputation as a pastry chef, which has led him to open his own 'show room' that clients can visit in order to choose the perfect tart, cake or pastry for special occasions. (Phone for an appointment if you're intrigued.) This historic building on the Ramblas, with interiors to match the fantastical façade also has a tea room where lesser mortals can enjoy a cup of coffee, chocolate or tea and some of Escribà's more accessible confectionery thrills. They also sell their own brand of chocolate and Cava. (You can taste an Escribà pastry dessert at their beachfront seafood restaurant, Xiringuito Escribà, see p. 57).

DRINK IN THE ATMOSPHERE

60 **Hotel España**

6 Carrer de Sant Pau, 9–11

Despite showing signs of being overvisited, the hotel designed by master Modernista architect Lluís Domènech i Montaner in 1902 is worth a stop for a drink and a look over the riot of decoration in the reception and restaurant spaces. Elaborate carved architectural details, vibrant tilework featuring floral motifs and intricate mosaic patterns and a five-metre-tall fireplace by sculptor Eusebi Arnau fill two rooms, while another formal dining room is enveloped in mythic sea murals by Ramon Casas, complete with frolicking fish and mermaids.

HARBOUR-SIDE DRINKS

42 La Miranda del Museu

35 Museu d'Història de Catalunya, Plaça de Pau Vila, 1

The museum itself occupies what were the general stores of the port of Barcelona, built at the end of the 19th century. However, the interior has had a complete modern overhaul, the crown of which is the terrace restaurant and bar on the fourth floor. After discovering the roots of Catalonian heritage (but there is no need to pay for entry to the museum if you're just going to the café), head upstairs for a very reasonable set lunch, drinks or à la carte dinner in a relaxed, contemporary setting with a fantastic view over the port and the city.

WINE AND SNACKS

42 La Vinya del Senyor

4 Plaça de Santa Maria, 5

With an angled view of Santa Maria del Mar, La Vinya del Senyor is a tiny, pleasant wine bar with relaxed attitude. Tucked away across the Plaça de Santa Maria, and under the management of Ramón Parellada (of Senyor Parellada, see p. 45), it's not an obvious tourist haunt but near enough to the centre to duck into for a taste of something special during a walk around the old city. A good and varied selection of around 300 native and imported wines, including Cava and Jerez, is served at the counter or at tables upstairs or down or on the ample outdoor terrace.

PARTY CENTRAL

42

Passeig del Born

23

- Pitín Bar, Passeig del Born, 34
- Plastic Bar, Passeig del Born, 19
- Borneo, Carrer del Rec, 49
- Gimlet, Carrer del Rec, 24

Opposite bright modern Sandwich & Friends (see p. 53) on the corner of Antic St Joan is the Pitín Bar, a well-established resident on this newly trendy block. This is definitely a night-time prospect, a small glassed-in corner space with shiny surfaces that fills up quickly and is usually packed after 11 or 12 at night. It has been around in some form since 1957, and despite the trendy feel still sells its specialty, *pitín*, a tea prepared in the same way as cappuccino with steamed milk instead of the poured stuff. A little way along the Passeig del Born on your right you will notice the orange glow emanating from the tunnel-shaped space before you see the sign for the Plastic Bar. Retro-style yellow-green patterns and the hanging silver stars and baubles reminiscent of Sputnik lamps are set off by the underlit orange plastic bar that makes everybody's drinks look like space juice but is still weirdly attractive. You'll no doubt be drawn into one or two of the many other haunts on this drinker's paradise of a street, but you'll want to explore the nearby Carrer del Rec, at the northern end of Passeig del Born, as well. The large-scale construction sites don't look very inviting, but this is the general state of things in an area that continues to up and come, and around the worksites the profusion of shops and bars continues unabated. Two of the more worthwhile drinking spots are Borneo, suffused with a groovy, world music vibe and friendly staff – sometimes you can't tell who is who as it all seems so relaxed. Gimlet, the original cocktail bar on the scene, pays homage to the classic New York bar of the 1940s, which must have something to do with the suit-clad barman, the well-dressed clients and jazz classics simmering over the hum of conversation. It's a seductive narrow wood-panelled space, and the bar itself is a substantial piece of warm, cherry-coloured wood, something you can lean against with confidence. They do serve gimlets, shaken, not stirred, and pretty much on the mark.

MODERN WINE AND TAPAS

80 CATA 1.81

25 Carrer de València, 181

They advertise 'vins, platillos & whisky', but the clean, modern interior suggests that this is no ordinary tapas and wine bar. It is in fact a new haven for oenophiles and of mini gastronomic surprises. There are more than 250 wines on offer by the bottle, with an emphasis on Spanish varieties, and a list of 25 by the glass that changes every 15 days. The small portions of contemporary Catalan cuisine are produced by chef Terésa Olivella, who also creates mini-hamburgers that have become, rather incongruously, a Cata trademark. Space is very limited so be there early.

COCKTAILS WITH GAUDÍ

80 La Pedrera at Night

34 Passeig de Gràcia, 92

If you happen to be visiting Barcelona in the summer months you will find that many places have extended hours and special terrace openings. One of the exceptional outdoor drinking experiences to be had is on the recently re-opened rooftop of Gaudí's Casa Milà/La Pedrera (see p. 93). The fanciful ventilation shafts, the irregular up-and-down pathways and eccentric little archways that make Gaudí's rooftop space a surreal wonderland become an incredibly atmospheric backdrop for cocktails on weekend evenings. You can sit and admire the architecture, gaze out toward the Sagrada Familia or down over the grand axis of Passeig de Gràcia and Carrer de Provença, or wave to your friends on the roof terrace of the Hotel Condes de Barcelona (see p. 124). Be advised, the steps can be hazardous after too many cocktails.

1940S CLUB STYLE

26 Ginger

Carrer de Palma de Sant Just, 1

This is one of the newer arrivals in the Barri Gòtic, but the style and feel are subtly retro. Its intimate seating arrangements on two, low-ceilinged levels with club chairs and other smart furnishings appeal to youthful, well-heeled drinkers, who come for the wide menu that features assorted cocktails and includes tacos, tapas and *tostadas* (hors d'oeuvre-style snacks on small toasted bread). More glamorous than your typical tapas bar, Ginger cultivates an intimate, sophisticated ambience of another era – down a back alley of Barcelona's medieval heart.

HAPHAZARD HARMONY

60 Merry Ant

28 Carrer del Peu de la Creu, 23

This bar certainly looks as if some giant of the species has been hard at work lugging in the collection of merry, mis-matched yet oddly coherent objects and then tacked together an assortment of wooden frames and shutters. It all makes for a jolly, arty sort of background, however, for the paintings and one-off lamps that are for sale around the room. The red lighting is part of the merry enchantment, as is the eclectic bohemian crowd and the well-priced drinks.

GREEN AND GROOVY

26 **Fonfone**

Carrer dels Escudellers, 24

A greenish glow can be more attractive than you might think. Fonfone is one of the most recent bars to enhance the hip-bohemian neighbourhood of the Escudellers. Like most Barcelona nightspots, its doors don't even open until 10 pm, and the locals don't start arriving until well after 11. No matter, earlier is a good time to take in the cool green upholstery, the walls filled with retro ovoid tiles in green and yellow and lamps made of simulated circuit boards. No wine is served, but all manner of cocktails, beer and DJ-spun music take the mood from chill to thrill.

CLUB TROPICANA

60 Salsitas

5 Carrer Nou de la Rambla, 22

Sculpted white pineapples and glass lamps filled with air bubbles light up the bar but there's more to come in the back dining room, where the plaster artists, under the direction of designers Rafael Tamborero and José Luis López, created palm trees with coconut lamps. Salsitas is an extraordinary example of the clubby bar-cum-restaurants that are springing up in Barcelona's hot spots. There is dining beneath the palms until midnight, when things get cleared out and the dancing starts in one of the Raval's most trippy-tropical clubs.

CLASSIC CERVECERIA

42 **El Vaso de Oro**

36 Carrer de Balboa, 6

There aren't too many places in Barcelona where beer holds sway over other drinks, but the 'golden glass' is probably at the top of the list. For those who like a good choice of brews – and one has to admit that it can go pretty well with tapas – El Vaso de Oro is a somewhat incongruous but necessary destination in fishy Barceloneta. With its old-style polished wood interior reminiscent of a captain's quarters and classic high-standard tapas that have no need to be flashy or innovative, the place is a favoured haunt for locals and visitors alike.

shop

In a city where many of the traditional crafts are still practised and where the word 'artisanal' is prominent in descriptions of everything from furnishings to gourmet produce, the temptations to buy are ubiquitous and well-argued. Where else will you get a jumper like the one you watched being woven in the Ribera? Where in the world can you get the selection of Iberian acorn-fed, cured ham, Catalan wines and cheeses? But save something for the designers, for although the top names may not have been globalized in the way their French and Italian counterparts have, Barcelona has a stellar international fashion nucleus. And of course Barcelona design is in a category of its own.

MASTER OF ACCESSORIES

42 Rafa Teja Atelier

16 Carrer de Santa Maria, 18

Rafael Teja has made a name for himself among the textile-loving population of the city with his handmade shawls, scarves, bags and wraps in a variety of weaves, colours and textures, from simple loose knits to plush angora. Although the shop features an odd assortment of Chinese-style silk jackets, it is Teja's range of intricate weaves in bold hues that are the real draw. Sturdy and stylish wool felt bags with wooden or tortoiseshell handles also have that one-off, hand-crafted appeal.

FINE NEW FASHIONS

60 Giménez & Zuazo

17 Raval: Carrer d'Elisabets, 20; El Born: Carrer del Rec, 42

From dainty lace dresses and printed velvet T-shirts to tailored patchwork skirt and trouser suits and fantastically bulky sweaters, Marta Giménez and Jorge Zuazo keep Barcelona bright and beautiful with their innovative use of striking fabrics and beautifully detailed designs. Their look is youthful but not as teen- or club-oriented as some of their fashion peers. Having met at the Barcelona school of fashion and technical arts, the pair had their first show at the Saló Gaudí in 1995 and have since gone from strength to strength, recently opening a second shop in the Born.

Josep Font

33 Carrer de Provença, 304

He's designed clothes for Barbie and collaborated on furniture with renowned architect Oscar Tusquets, but he is still one of Barcelona's most exciting women's fashion designers. Though he has expanded to shops in Madrid, Bilbao and most recently in the Faubourg St Honoré in Paris, Josep Font is a Barcelona native. He studied fashion here at the International Fashion Institute and his headquarters is still here, though his reputation has spread well beyond regional boundaries and he's been honoured with awards from Balenciaga, L'Oréal, *Elle* and Moët et Chandon, among a host of others. But go to his Carrer de Provença shop for an up-close look at the long, lean dresses with ruffled hemlines and tailored, draping trousers as well as an assortment of other slim and sexy items in bold colours. You'll even find people hanging around outside just to look through the neoclassical portal at Font's eye-catching Baroque minimal interiors.

OLD SOFT SHOES

26 La Manual Alpargatera

Carrer d'Avinyó, 7

What do Catherine Zeta-Jones, Michael Douglas, Jack Nicholson, Juan Antonio Samaranch and the Pope have in common? They all own espadrilles from La Manual Alpargatera, and this is the only place to get a pair for yourself. The shop began as a workshop, which opened just after the Civil War and continues to provide locals (many of whom have customary yearly 'appointments') as well as foreigners with the traditional and highly eco-friendly footwear that has been around in some form for thousands of years. (For anyone who doesn't already know, espadrilles are the ideal thing for walking over cobblestones, provided, of course, that it doesn't rain.) The distinctive white shopfront has become a Barcelona landmark, so the place is no well-kept secret, but don't let the tourists put you off: these shoes are the genuine article.

ARTISANAL LEATHER

80 Muxart

30 Carrer del Roselló, 230

Barcelona shoe designer Hermenegildo Muxart began making his own brand of men's and women's footwear in 1989 and has become known for his particular wild and wonderful combinations of colour and design in leather and suede in shoes, boots, handbags and jackets. The quality and cut of material are made noticeable with tightly fitting ankle boots in deep red or burgundy or court shoes with a diamond pattern of different-coloured leather. Muxart favours leather that looks creamy or with a slightly crackled polish. Combinations of black and red are favourites, as are chunky seams and accented stitching. In Spain, the land of leather, Muxart makes his own distinctive statement and it's set to spread far and wide.

ART NOUVEAU JEWELRY

80 Bagués Masriera

13 Passeig de Gràcia, 41

Lluís Masriera (1872–1958) brought the Art Nouveau style to fine jewelry. His pieces became known throughout the world, as did the techniques he developed, such as 'Barcelona enamel', a translucent and highly luminous material. He established his own company in 1839, which has continued to produce his designs ever since: sinuous sea nymphs, dynamic floral motifs, delicate winged creatures. The company has grown and diversified (merging with Bagués in 1985), but the Masriera pieces are still as potent, and the whole collection is housed in two significant Modernista buildings, of which the Casa Amatller, designed by Josep Puig i Cadafalch in 1900, is the most important. The interior has wonderful Modernista-style woodwork and furnishings. The public courtyard entrance features stained glass and metalwork lamps in the signature dragon designs and there is a *sala d'exposicios* upstairs, separate from the jewelry shop, which allows a look inside the building.

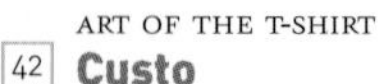

ART OF THE T-SHIRT

42 Custo

13 Plaça de les Olles, 7

Brothers Custo and David Dalmau started this wild psychedelic label after being inspired by California surfwear during a worldwide motorcycle tour in the 1980s. Now they are among the top names in clubwear, with a collection of racy and colourful prints and patterns that might make your head spin if they weren't so beguiling. Julia Roberts, Penelope Cruz, Michael Stipe and the Backstreet Boys are among the celebrities who have sported their super-trendy designs. For something of a knockout on the dance floors of Barcelona, Ibiza or anywhere else, grab a little T-shirt, top, skirt or trousers and mix and match with abandon.

MILLINER WITH FLAIR

26 **Nina Pawlowsky**

Carrer de Nou Sant Francesc, 17

Nina Pawlowsky began her career as a costume designer for theatre, film and television and she continues to keep herself at a frantic pace creating designs for productions like *The Magic Flute*, *Guys and Dolls*, *Oedipus Rex* and, most recently, *Romeo and Juliet*, for venues like the Gran Teatre del Liceu (see p. 67). Her tiny shop on the Carrer Nou de Sant Francesc in the Barri Gòtic is a jewel box full of her fanciful ex-theatre creations that feature theatrical flourishes. But they are also very modern and demonstrate a sophisticated touch. A variety of fanciful styles includes delicate swirls that perch at the top of the forehead, a very louche red silk cloche and a stripy woven stove-pipe number. Her designs can also usually be seen in exhibitions around the city.

AVANT-GARDE DESIGN OUTLET

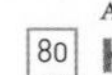

80 **Hipòtesi**

29 Rambla de Catalunya, 105

Designed in 1997 by Pilar Vila, the cool, ordered space set somewhat anonymously in the far reaches of the Eixample shows off some of Barcelona's most talented new designers in jewelry, textiles, ceramics and other artisanal crafts. The minimal, concrete interior is a calm backdrop for the highest-quality one-off and limited-edition pieces by Spanish and international designers as well. An intimate and accessible forum, Hipòtesi is known for leading the way in new design and regularly hosts exhibitions of work by makers from around the world.

FASHION FAVOURITE

80 Antonio Miro

14 Carrer del Consell de Cent, 349

A well-established name in the Spanish fashion world, Miro opened the store Groc in 1968 to sell his own designs. Now Groc sells an array of Spanish and international designers, while Miro, who created an international brand in the early 1980s and was presented with the Balenciaga design award in 1988, has his own outlets. He has since opened Miro Jeans, licensed designs under Muxart shoes (see p. 165) and designed the uniforms for the Spanish Olympic team in 1992. He also designed the interiors for the beautifully minimal Hotel Miro, which opened in early 2003. His clothes are sold worldwide but this shop in his Catalan homeland, designed by Miro with architect Pilar Líbano in 1995 (see also Lydia Delgado, next page), houses the full range of his new collections for men and women. Expect slim, tailored lines and exciting fabrics, as he is known for his attention to texture and weave.

MASTERFULLY WOVEN

80 **David Valls**

10 Carrer de València, 235

Like many Catalan designers, David Valls has a reputation for using interesting textiles. But he goes even further in creating or altering some of the cloth himself by weaving, dyeing or other treatments. The result is a collection of colours and fabrics you won't see anywhere else. Sensuous and inspired, using an artisanal but supremely elegant touch, Valls's shop in the Eixample is a seductive space designed by Pere Puig, with lots of ambient lighting to enhance his tunic-style sweaters, long dresses and other luxurious knits.

TRIM AND TAILORED

96 **Lydia Delgado**

12 Carrer de Minerva, 21

Her style has been likened to Audrey Hepburn but Lydia Delgado does much more than trimly tailored feminine suits. After trekking up a narrow street of characterless buildings, her green-tinged retail space hung with draperies and gilt-framed mirrors – created with the help of architect Pilar Líbano – is a real find. Delgado's latest designs, from her signature perfume-bottle-print silk separates to her brushed corduroy striped suits in deep purple and red and velvety long jackets with rose appliqués to her classic wool coats, exude fashion with substance.

TACTILE BEAUTY

42 Mar Rodriguez

6 Carrer dels Mirallers, 7, Local 1

A designer who takes the local tradition of handwoven textiles and applies it with stunning modern style, Mar Rodriguez makes comfortable, loose-fitting but superbly chic designs for men and women. She began showing her collections only after completing her studies in fashion design in 1999, but the prizes have come thick and fast, such as that of 'young Spanish designer of the year' at the Gaudí fashion shows of 2002. This is her first and only outlet, but she is sure to be a hit among those who like tactile beauty. Her clothes in linen and wool or cotton knit are a refined take on the textile tradition, with sleeveless tunics and blousy drawstring trousers for men and women, and imaginative halter tops and short skirts, all in a range, from unusual vivid colours to soft, neutral tones. Exploring methods of weaving, dyeing and tinting, as well as hand-crafting her fabrics, she brings together, in basic natural materials, a profusion of textures, contrasts and colours that is thoroughly modern.

THE DESIGNERS' OUTLET

42 On Land

11 Carrer de la Princesa, 25

Along the Carrer de la Princesa, which is mostly full of small shops stuffed with gadgets and imported novelty items, On Land definitely stands out. As a source for local design talent, this is the cutting-edge Barcelona fashion institution. With another shop in the Eixample (Valencia 273), it stocks the latest, most exciting designer wear of the city and beyond for men and women who care about original design. This is, for example, the only local outlet for the collection of young Josep Abril, who has caused a stir in the fashion pages with his street-wise urban wear. Other designers included in the fresh-looking, brightly painted spaces are Anaya, Giménez & Zuazo (see p. 162), Montse Ibañez, Hergenhahn knitwear and the shop's own label.

WE SHOULD ALL HAVE THEM

80 Bad Habits

11 Carrer de València, 261

The shop windows offer only an enticing glimpse through a low doorway and usually displays something that looks like the goods of a fetish den but this is actually the outlet of Mireya Ruiz, one of the city's most acclaimed designers. Ruiz started out selling second-hand clothes (many of which she found in markets in Amsterdam and London) in the Plaça del Sol but soon began adding her own touches. Now she carries her own original creations, which have garnered her appreciation in the fashion press and the confidence of other Spanish designers whose clothing she also sells in her ultra-modern shop. Her collection features experiments with texture and form, from edgy street designs to close-fitting, sexy ensembles in a mixture of natural and new fabrics.

HOME OF DESIGN

80

BD: Ediciones de Diseño

21 Carrer de Mallorca, 291

This mecca for modern design was founded in Barcelona in 1972 by a group of designers because, as they say, 'nobody was daring enough to put our ideas into production'. So Oscar Tusquets, Pep Bonet, Cristian Cirici and Lluís Clotet started their own company, which has become the city's pre-eminent design source. It helps that they found Lluís Domènech i Montaner's Casa Thomas in which to house their work, itself a classic piece of architectural history. BD made their own history being, as they call themselves, 'design publishers', sourcing different manufacturers to aid in their two-pronged approach, which involves reproducing classic pieces by everyone from Gaudí and Dalí to Charles Rennie Mackintosh while producing the work of new Spanish and international designers. Among these is Javier Mariscal, who is best known for creating 'Cobi', the mascot for the summer Olympics of 1992, and for his trendy restaurant (see Tragaluz, p.90) and dance-club interiors, but who has gone on to become one of the city's premier designers.

OENOPHILE'S DELIGHT

42 **Vila Viniteca**

18 Carrer dels Agullers, 7

This is a serious wine lover's paradise. With over 3000 wines and liqueurs, including some fantastic unexported discoveries from the Catalan region, Vila Viniteca is where many citydwellers (including some of the better restaurants) go to source bottles of quality. The staff are very knowledgeable and helpful, and some of them can explain the Spanish regions and varieties in English. Of particular note among the walls and cellars of stock, especially for visitors, are wines from the tiny, emerging Catalonian region Priorat, which produces very high-quality reds. Try a bottle of Les Terrasses for a start.

MONASTERY MADE

14 **Caelum**

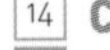

5 Carrer de la Palla, 8

Caelum is a unique shop with a window on the v-shaped corner of Carrer de Palla and Banys Nous, surrounded by antiques dealers. It sells solely the produce of monasteries and convents mostly in Spain, though they do stock some beauty products made in the monastery of Santa Maria Novella in Milan (there is a shop devoted to their products, at Carrer Espaseria, 4–8). Some 38 monasteries and convents around Spain craft the many teas, cakes, biscuits, toffees, chocolates, crackers and preserves, as well as candles and soaps with images of angels inside. All are tastefully packaged and would make very distinctive gifts if you can manage to part with them. There is also a café that serves cakes and teas and is open most of the day. Downstairs is the real treat, where between the bare stone walls of the 14th-century crypt (which you can spy through the grille in the floor when you enter the shop) more tables are set out in a tea shop that opens at 4 pm. A large assortment of the products sold in the shop is served.

ROASTED DELIGHTS

42 E & A Gispert

12 Carrer dels Sombrerers, 23

From the quaint wood-fronted shop and the woodcut logo to the wooden barrels full of roasted aromatic nuts and coffee and the shelves full of nicely wrapped treats, E & A Gispert is a delight for the senses. What began in 1851 as a small family business started by Josep Gispert with his sons, Enric and Alfons, was finally sold in 1993 to the two brothers, who continue the tradition of roasting and drying their own fruits, nuts and coffee on the premises in what is reputedly the only Roman-style log oven still used in Europe. In addition, the brothers have expanded the range of natural products from around Catalunya as well as the rest of Spain. Chocolate, honey, olive oil, fruit and vegetable preserves, regional sweets such as the popular Alicante, which resembles almonds in nougat, are sold along with their own brand of coffee, chocolate and nuts. Awarded the Coq d'Or by Les Gourmands Associés of France in 1999, E & A Gispert really is a unique Barcelona delicacy.

CHOCOLATE FANTASY

14 Xocoa

7 Carrer d'En Bot, 4

Along Carrer de Petritxol you'll find the café (serving desserts such as fig ravioli) and the smaller version of the chocolate boutique. But Xocoa's newest and largest boutique is on the tiny Carrer d'En Bot. Though they have expanded to three shops, Xocoa is still a uniquely Barcelonan enterprise. Their more than two dozen kinds of chocolate bars and selection of filled chocolates are all made here to their own recipe. Bars of chocolate range from the slightly familiar *arroz inflado* ('puffed rice') and one with a pleasantly bitter coffee flavour, to the more exotic pistachio, green tea and thyme flavours. In addition, for hardcore cocoa addicts they have bars ranging in percentage of cocoa solids from 52 (already above your average 'dark' chocolate bar) to 73 or even 90. They have white and milk chocolate bars and bars without sugar, boxed chocolates, pastries and biscuits topped with dried fruits and nuts, chocolate CDs and keys, all in a brightly minimal space with funky retro-style packaging. Willy Wonka, eat your heart out.

EXOTIC CHOCOLATES

80 Cacao Sampaka

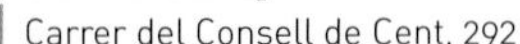

7 Carrer del Consell de Cent, 292

It will soon become clear when you start wandering around Barcelona that the Catalans have a real and multilayered love affair with chocolate in all its forms. From a cream-topped *suizo* (see Granja Dulcinea, p. 148) to a chocolate dessert that features savoury seasonings, chocolate is more than a treat, it's a gastronomic staple. Cacao Sampaka, rather than posing as a mere chocolate vendor, is a journey through the history and culture of chocolate around the world. And lest this prove too abstract for the munching public, the store made itself welcome with the inauguration of a new springtime tradition: on 21 March they bring out a chocolate egg weighing 400 kilos and invite members of the public to help hack it into bite-sized bits. But this is only a prelude to what is inside: chocolates in flavours you would never have imagined or dreamed of enjoying: from the tame fruit and nut collection, featuring almonds, sesame, pine nuts or orange pieces, to the 'Spices of America' collection, which is infused with vanilla, cinnamon, curry or saffron, or the 'Flowers and Herbs', of violet-, rose-, lavender- or jasmine-enhanced morsels. There are also truffles, liqueur-filled chocolates, biscuits and solid bars in a variety of densities. The beautifully spare shop interior full of dark, chocolate-coloured wood was designed by Antoni Arola and features a café in the back where you can sample chocolate drinks and gourmet pastries.

retreat

Who needs to retreat from Barcelona? It's better to think of getting out of the city as an enhancement of the Catalan experience via mountains, forests, vineyards and beaches. Overlooked by majestic peaks, skirted by fruitful plains and facing an appealing coastline, Barcelona is the base for adventures ranging from serious mountain trekking to serious sun splashing, from clubbing and wine-tasting to dining in some of the country's and possibly the world's most exquisite restaurants. All are less than a two-hour drive from the city, so it would be a shame to miss out on several enchanting accommodations that feel worlds away.

El Racó de
Can Fabes

SCALING THE HEIGHTS

Montseny: Mountain and Culinary Peaks

- Montseny mountain trail
- El Racó de Can Fabes
- Hotel Sant Marçal

Only 10 kilometres or so northwest of the city of Barcelona, the terrain becomes mountainous and thickly forested. The National Park of Montseny is the perfect place to trek in tree-covered foothills. Of course the more adventurous hiker will consider taking on a climb of Tagamanent (1055 metres) or Turo de l'Home (1712 metres). But before embarking on a tour of the forests and spa towns for which this region is famous you might want to get settled in a suitably rugged but pleasantly luxurious accommodation. Although the Hotel Sant Marçal is no rustic shelter, it is housed in 11th-century monastery buildings that are up a narrow road and retain much of their stone and wood charm, not to mention being a cosy place to revive after a good long walk. A relaxing swim in the pool has the added benefit of a spectacular mountain vista. All good preparation for an unforgettable meal at one of Spain's finest restaurants, which just happens to be down the (rather winding) road. Santi Santamaria is the chef at El Racó de Can Fabes, which he started in an old stone country house before catapulting to international acclaim. Should you manage to get a table (booked well in advance) you will be treated to a three-Michelin-star meal by the self-taught chef, who is challenging French dominion over world gastronomy using hand-selected local ingredients to create his highly satisfying Catalonian haute cuisine.

Figueres and Environs: The Surreal Experience

- Dalí house and museum
- El Bulli Restaurant
- Hotel Mas Falgarona

This is a journey that combines fantastic food with a fantastical setting: a trip to Figueres, the home of Salvador Dalí, combined with dinner in the coastal town of Rosas at El Bulli, considered one of the world's best and most innovative restaurants. Chef Ferran Adrià has become a legend in his own time, and his restaurant (open only from April to September) is booked several months in advance. A native of Barcelona, Adrià has made his name with things like orange caviar, egg-yolk tempura, foamy vegetable mousse and desserts that feature sweet and savoury flavours bursting together with pop rocks and slightly solidified espresso. In 20 years, he has, it is safe to say, reinvented haute cuisine. Before dinner, visit the Teatre-Museu Dalí, which has lighting and even music designed by Dalí as well as some of his trademark dreamscapes. Next door, the house with the eggs on top is where Dalí resided while his wife often stayed in the medieval Castell Gala, 25 miles (40 kilometres) south of the city in Púbol. His other residence in the charming seaside village of Cadaqués is worth a visit for the winding little cobbled streets and lovely beach as much as the little house, which can take only a limited number of visitors.

Complete the experience with a stay at the Mas Falgarona, a *mas*, or farmhouse, that was first registered in 1098, before the little town of Avínyonet de Puigventós was settled. It now comprises a 19-room hotel about 5 miles (3 kilometres) outside of Figueres. Severino Jallas Gándara and Brigitta Schmidt have 45 years' hotel experience between them and worked in a top hotel in Switzerland before buying this property in 1999 and bringing the medieval stone buildings to a state of rustic elegance. The interiors are dominated by stone walls, low arches and wood beams offset by crisp, white linens in the bedrooms and bright *azulejos* in the bathrooms. The outdoor swimming pool is surrounded by shrubs and palms. Schmidt cooks for the restaurant using 'the best products from the mountains and the sea', so the menu is always changing but always fresh.

HILLTOP SANCTUARY

Cardona: Medieval Romance

Catalunya is ringed by imposing fortresses and monasteries, and one of the most popular excursions is to Montserrat, the monastery dedicated to the 'Black Virgin', which is a fascinating medieval complex with panoramic views in an incomparable setting. However, for a less populous and more romantic experience, you can continue another 35 miles (50 kilometres), toward Andorra to the ancient salt-mining settlement of Cardona (about 55 miles [85 kilometres] from Barcelona). Here you have not only the chance to visit the 11th-century chapel and majestic castle, but also to stay in the castle itself. Well visible from miles away on its strategic perch overlooking the valley, with a series of towers all huddled together behind massive protective walls, the Parador del Cardona is a 9th-century fortification turned luxury accommodation, a destination that will take you far from the crowds and into a secluded, historic embrace. From the castle grounds you look out on to vast protected forests and little towns strung along the river Cardoner. Inside the castle hotel are stone walls, most in the public areas painted a deep, alluring crimson. The preserved Gothic arches and bare stone are softened with medieval-style furnishings, such as dark wood chairs with dark velvet coverings. Some rooms feature four-poster beds hung with gauzy bed curtains. There are, of course modern elements, and all rooms feature up-to-the-minute modern conveniences. The buildings themselves are an architectural-historical wonder. Built in the distinctive solidity of the Catalan Gothic style complete with a protective moat, the castle retains an aura of proud resistance. The oldest section, the Minyona Tower, dates from the 2nd century and together with the thousand-year-old chapel is a vivid lesson in Catalan heritage. When you descend into the town below, you can visit the ancient saline mountain, or Montaña de Sal Gema, and Roman-era salt mines. You might take advantage of the cafés, but the hotel has its own restaurant set within the stone arches that serves good-quality Catalan cuisine.

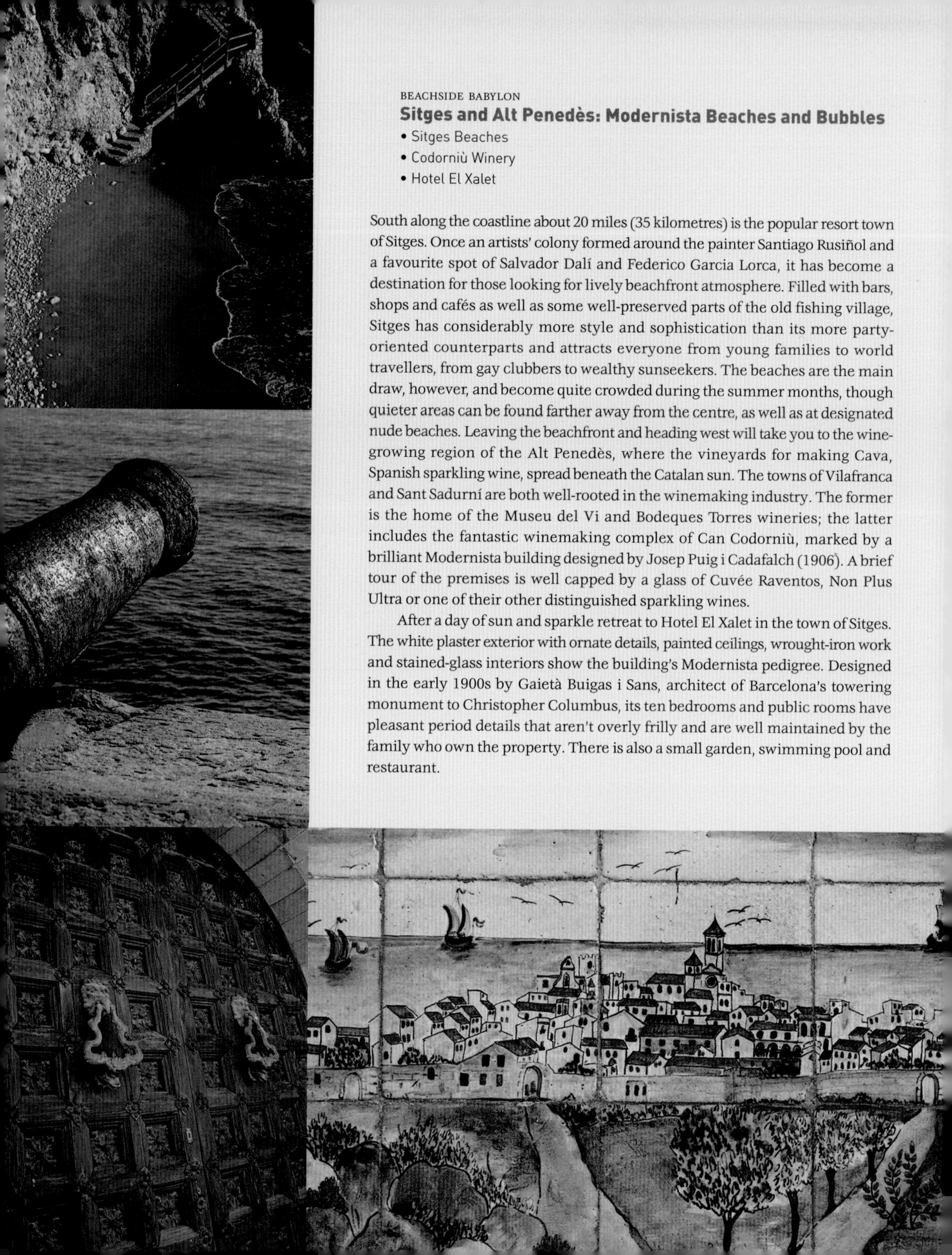

BEACHSIDE BABYLON

Sitges and Alt Penedès: Modernista Beaches and Bubbles

- Sitges Beaches
- Codorniù Winery
- Hotel El Xalet

South along the coastline about 20 miles (35 kilometres) is the popular resort town of Sitges. Once an artists' colony formed around the painter Santiago Rusiñol and a favourite spot of Salvador Dalí and Federico Garcia Lorca, it has become a destination for those looking for lively beachfront atmosphere. Filled with bars, shops and cafés as well as some well-preserved parts of the old fishing village, Sitges has considerably more style and sophistication than its more party-oriented counterparts and attracts everyone from young families to world travellers, from gay clubbers to wealthy sunseekers. The beaches are the main draw, however, and become quite crowded during the summer months, though quieter areas can be found farther away from the centre, as well as at designated nude beaches. Leaving the beachfront and heading west will take you to the wine-growing region of the Alt Penedès, where the vineyards for making Cava, Spanish sparkling wine, spread beneath the Catalan sun. The towns of Vilafranca and Sant Sadurní are both well-rooted in the winemaking industry. The former is the home of the Museu del Vi and Bodeques Torres wineries; the latter includes the fantastic winemaking complex of Can Codorniù, marked by a brilliant Modernista building designed by Josep Puig i Cadafalch (1906). A brief tour of the premises is well capped by a glass of Cuvée Raventos, Non Plus Ultra or one of their other distinguished sparkling wines.

After a day of sun and sparkle retreat to Hotel El Xalet in the town of Sitges. The white plaster exterior with ornate details, painted ceilings, wrought-iron work and stained-glass interiors show the building's Modernista pedigree. Designed in the early 1900s by Gaietà Buigas i Sans, architect of Barcelona's towering monument to Christopher Columbus, its ten bedrooms and public rooms have pleasant period details that aren't overly frilly and are well maintained by the family who own the property. There is also a small garden, swimming pool and restaurant.

contact

All telephone numbers are given for dialling locally. From abroad, the country code is +34, followed by the number below. Telephone numbers in the retreat section are given for dialling from Barcelona: if calling from abroad, dial the country code plus the number given. The number in brackets by the name is the page number on which the entry appears.

Abac [132]
Carrer del Rec 79–89
08003 Barcelona
T 93 319 66 00
F 93 319 45 19
E abac12@telefonica.net
W www.restaurantaba.biz

Again(st) [34]
Carrer del Palau, 6
08002 Barcelona
T/F 93 301 54 52
E info@againstbcn.com
W www.againstbcn.com

Agut [37]
Carrer d'En Gignàs, 16
08002 Barcelona
T 93 315 17 09

Anamorfosis [22]
Carrer Santa Eulalia, 4
08002 Barcelona
T 93 301 29 43

Antigüedades [22]
Carrer de Banys Nous, 17a
08002 Barcelona

Antonio Miro [168]
Carrer del Consell de Cent 349
08007 Barcelona
T 93 487 06 70
F 93 467 71 11

Antonio Pernas [86]
Carrer del Consell de Cent, 314–16
08007 Barcelona
T 93 487 16 67

L'Arca de l'Àvia [22]
Carrer de Banys Nous, 20
08002 Barcelona
T/F 93 302 15 98

Atalanta Manufactura [47]
Passeig del Born, 10
08003 Barcelona
T 93 268 37 02

Bad Habits [171]
Carrer de València, 261
08007 Barcelona
T 93 487 22 59

Bagués Masriera [166]
Passeig de Gràcia, 41
08007 Barcelona
T 93 216 01 74
F 93 487 70 01
La Rambla, 105
08002 Barcelona
T 93 481 70 50
F 93 302 49 30)
E info@bagues.es

La Balsa [108]
Carrer Infanta Isabel, 4
08022 Barcelona
T 93 211 50 48
F 93 418 46 06

Bar del Pi [21]
Plaça de Sant Josep Oriol, 1
08002 Barcelona
T 93 302 21 23

BD: Ediciones de Diseño [172]
Carrer de Mallorca, 291
08037 Barcelona
T 93 458 69 09
F 93 207 36 97
W www.bdbarcelona.com

Bestiari [54]
Carrer del Comerç, 25
T 93 268 30 80

Biblioteca [64]
Carrer de Junta de Comerç 28
08001 Barcelona
T 93 412 62 21

Bodega La Palma [37]
Carrer de Palma de Sant Just, 7
08002 Barcelona
T 93 315 06 56

La Bodegueta del Xampú [82]
Gran Via de les Corts Catalanes, 702
08010 Barcelona
T 93 265 04 83

Borneo [152]
Carrer del Rec, 49
08003 Barcelona
T 93 268 23 89

Botafumeíro [103]
Carrer Gran de Gràcia, 81
08012 Barcelona
T 93 218 42 30/93 217 96 42

Cacao Sampaka [175]
Carrer del Consell de Cent, 292
08007 Barcelona
T 93 272 08 33
E info@cacaosampaka.com
W www.cacaosampaka.com

Caelum [173]
Carrer de la Palla, 8
08002 Barcelona
T 93 302 69 93

Cafè de l'Academia [37]
Carrer de Lledó, 1
08002 Barcelona
T 93 319 82 53

Café del Sol [100]
Plaça del Sol, 16
08012 Barcelona
T 93 415 56 63

Café Salambo [99]
Carrer de Torrijos, 51
08012 Barcelona
T 93 218 69 66

Ca l'Isidre [145]
Carrer de Les Flors, 12
08001 Barcelona
T 93 441 11 39
F 93 442 52 71

Can Solé [57]
Carrer de Sant Carles, 4
08003 Barcelona
T 93 221 50 12

Can Travi Nou [136]
Carrer Jorge Manrique
08035 Barcelona
T 93 428 03 01
F 93 428 19 17
W www.barcelonarestaurant.com

Capella de la Merced [104]
Carrer de Laforja, 17
08006 Barcelona

Carmelitas [68]
Carrer del Doctor Dou,1 /
Carme, 42
08001 Barcelona
T 93 412 46 84

Casa Almirall [73]
Carrer de Joaquín Costa, 33
08001 Barcelona
T 93 412 15 35

Casa Batlló [86]
Passeig de Gràcia, 43
08007 Barcelona
T 93 488 06 66

Casa Calvet [134]
Carrer de Casp, 48
08010 Barcelona
T 93 412 40 12
F 93 412 43 36
E rbmesa@softly.es
W www.gulliver.es/
casacalvet.htm

Casa Leopoldo [130]
Carrer Sant Rafael 24
08001 Barcelona
T 93 441 30 14

Casals Pagès [85]
Carrer de Roger de Llúria, 7
08010 Barcelona
T 93 343 79 00
F 93 342 47 42
E info@casalspages.com
W www.casalspages.com

**Casa Milà/
La Pedrera** [93/155]
Passeig de Gràcia 92
08008 Barcelona
T 93 484 59 00

Casa Oliveras [38]
Carrer de Dagueria, 11
08002 Barcelona
T 93 315 19 05

Casa Vicens [103]
Carrer de les Carolines, 24
08012 Barcelona

Castell de Montjuïc – Museu Militar [77]
Ctra Montjuïc, 62-68
08038 Barcelona
T 93 329 86 13
F 93 329 86 13

CATA 1.81 [154]
Carrer de València, 181
08011 Barcelona
T 93 323 68 18
E cata181@hotmail.com

Catedral de Barcelona [16]
Plaça de la Seu, 3
08002 Barcelona
T 93 315 15 54
F 93 310 10 46
W www.catedralbcn.org

La Cocotte [53]
Passeig del Born, 16
08003 Barcelona
T 93 319 17 34

Colibrí [73]
Carrer de la Riera Alta, 33–35
08001 Barcelona
T 93 443 23 06

Comerç 24 [139]
Carrer del Comerç, 24
08003 Barcelona
T 319 21 02

**Cooperativa
d'Arquitectes** [16]
Plaça Nova, 5
08002 Barcelona
T 93 481 35 60
F 93 481 35 61

Custo [166]
Plaça de les Olles, 7
08003 Barcelona
T 93 268 78 93
W www.custo-barcelona.com

David Valls [169]
Carrer de València 235
08007 Barcelona
T 93 487 1285

De Lis [104]
Carrer del Comte de
Salvatierra, 10 bis
08006 Barcelona
T 93 416 10 95
E delis@menta.net

Drolma [135]
Passeig de Gràcia 68
08007 Barcelona
T 93 496 77 10
F 93 488 18 80

E & A Gispert [174]
Carrer dels Sombrerers, 23
08003 Barcelona
T 93 319 75 35
F 93 319 71 71
E casagispert@casagispert.com
W www.casagispert.com

Edison's [73]
Carrer de la Riera Baixa, 9
08001 Barcelona
T 93 441 96 74
F 93 329 23 15
W www.discos-edisons.com

Erretè [73]
Carrer de la Riera Baixa, 10
08001 Barcelona
T 93 929 62 00

Escribà [149]
Rambla de les Flors, 83
08002 Barcelona
T/F 93 301 60 27
W www.escriba.es

**Església Santa Maria
del Mar** [45]
Plaça de Santa Maria, 1/
Passeig del Born
08003 Barcelona
T 93 310 23 90

**Església Santa Maria
del Pi** [22]
Plaça del Pi/Plaça de Sant
Josep Oriol
08002 Barcelona

Espai Baroque [50]
Palau Dalmeses
Carrer de Montcada, 20
08003 Barcelona
T 93 310 06 73

**Espai Sucre
(Escola Restaurant
des Postres)** [138]
Carrer de la Princesa 53
08003 Barcelona
T 93 268 16 30
F 93 268 15 23
E espaisucre@teleline.es
W www.espaisucre.com

Espai Vidre [70]
Fundació Centre del
Vidre de Barcelona
Carrer dels Àngels, 8
08001 Barcelona
T/F 93 318 98 33
E vidrebcn@fcv-bcn.org
W www.fcv-bcn.org

La Estrella de Plata [141]
Plaça del Palau, 13
08003 Barcelona
T 93 319 60 07

Estudi Tèxtil del Born [46]
Carrer de Brosolí, 1 local 4
08003 Barcelona
T 93 319 84 51
E etb@bluedeep.net

Fonfone [157]
Carrer dels Escudellers, 24
08002 Barcelona
T 93 317 14 24
W www.fonfone.com

Forum Ferlandina [71]
Carrer de Ferlandina, 31
08001 Barcelona
T 93 441 80 18
W www.forvmjoies.com

Fundació Antoni Tàpies [87]
Carrer d'Aragó 255
08007 Barcelona
T 93 487 03 15
F 93 487 00 09
E museu@ftapies.com

Fundació Joan Miró [77]
Parc de Montjuïc
08038 Barcelona
T 93 443 94 70
F 93 329 86 09
E fjmiro@bcn.fjmiro.es
W www.bcn.fjmiro.es

Futura [33]
Carrer dels Escudellers, 56
08002 Barcelona
T 93 317 49 75

Gaig [108]
Passeig de Maragall, 402
08031 Barcelona
T 93 429 10 17
F 93 429 70 02
E gaig@horta-bcn.com

**Galería Estrany
de la Mota** [90]
Passatge de Mercader, 18
08008 Barcelona
T 93 215 70 51
F 93 487 35 52
E galeria@estranydelamota.com
W www.estranydelamota.com

Galeria Joan Prats [85]
Rambla de Catalunya, 54
08007 Barcelona

T 93 216 02 84
F 93 487 1614
E galeria@galeriajoanprats.com
W www.galeriajoanprats.com

Galeria Maeght [50]
Carrer de Montcada, 25
08003 Barcelona
T 93 310 42 45
F 93 310 6 09
E maeghtbarcelona@intermail.es

Gemma Povo [22]
Carrer de Banys Nous 5–7
T 93 301 34 76
F 93 318 01 44
E gemmapovo@gemmapovo.com
W www.gemmapovo-bcn.com

Giardinetto [104]
Carrer de la Granada del Penedès, 22
08006 Barcelona
T 93 218 75 36

Giménez & Zuazo [162]
Carrer d'Elisabets, 20
08001 Barcelona
T 93 412 33 81
Carrer del Rec, 42
08003 Barcelona

Gimlet [152]
Carrer del Rec, 24
08003 Barcelona
T 93 310 10 27

Ginger [156]
Carrer de Palma de Sant Just, 1/
Carrer de Lledó, 2
08002 Barcelona
T 93 310 53 09

Gotham [34]
Carrer de Cervantes, 7
08002 Barcelona
T/F 93 412 46 47
W www.gotham-bcn.com

Grand Teatre del Liceu [67]
La Rambla, 51–59
08002 Barcelona
T 93 485 99 00
F 93 485 99 18
E informacio@liceubarcelona.com
W www.liceubarcelona.com

Granja Dulcinea [148]
Carrer de Petritxol 2
08002 Barcelona
T 93 302 68 24

Granja M. Viader [67]
Carrer d'En Xuclà, 4-6
08001 Barcelona
T 93 318 34 86

Grus Watch [16]
El Triangle, Carrer Pelai 39
08001 Barcelona
T 93 302 41 88
W www.gruswatch.com

Halagos [89]
Carrer de València, 189
08011 Barcelona
T 93 452 55 28
F 93 452 55 29
E foie@halagos2001.com
W www.halagos2001.com

Harlem Jazz Club [33]
Carrer de la Comtessa de Sobradiel, 8
08002 Barcelona
T 93 310 07 55

Herboristeria del Rei [29]
Carrer del Vidre, 1
08002 Barcelona
T 93 318 05 12

Hipòtesi [167]
Rambla de Catalunya, 105
08008 Barcelona
T 93 215 02 98/93 487 06 83

Hofmann [135]
Carrer de l'Argentería 74–78
08003 Barcelona
T/F 93 319 58 89
W www.hofmann-bcn.com

Hostal Gat Raval [122]
Carrer de Joaquín Costa, 44,
2nd Floor
08001 Barcelona
T 93 481 66 70
F 93 342 66 97
E hostalgatraval@gataccommodation.com
W www.gataccommodation.com

Hotel Banys Orientals [120]
Carrer de l'Argenteria, 37
08003 Barcelona
T 93 268 84 60
F 93 268 84 61
W www.hotelbanysorientals.com

Hotel Condes de Barcelona [124]
Passeig de Gràcia, 73–75
08008 Barcelona
T 93 467 47 80
F 93 467 47 81
E condesbcn@condesdebarcelona.com
W www.condesdebarcelona.com

Hotel España [150]
Carrer de Sant Pau 9–11
08001 Barcelona
T 93 318 17 58
F 93 317 11 34
E hotelespanya@hotelespanya.com
W www.hotelespanya.com

Hotel Mesón Castilla [118]
Carrer de Valldonzella, 5
08001 Barcelona
T 93 318 21 82
F 93 412 40 20
E hmesoncastilla@teleline.es
W www.mesoncastilla.com

Hotel Turó de Vilana [116]
Carrer de Vilana, 7
08017 Barcelona
T 93 434 03 63
F 93 418 89 03
E hotel@turodevilana.com
W www.turodevilana.com

Jamboree [29]
Plaça Reial, 17
08002 Barcelona
T 93 319 17 89
F 93 315 02 21
E jamboree@masimas.com
W www.masimas.com

Jardi Botànic [77]
Carrer Doctor Font i Quer
Parc de Montjuïc
08038 Barcelona
T 93 426 49 35
F 93 424 50 53
W oliba.uoc.edu/jardi_botanic/index2.html

Jean Luc Figueras [144]
Carrer de Santa Teresa, 10
08012 Barcelona
T 93 415 28 77

Joaquín Berao [88]
Carrer del Roselló, 227
08008 Barcelona
T 93 218 61 87
W www.joaquinberao.com

Josep Font [163]
Carrer de Provença, 304
08008 Barcelona
T 93 487 21 19
E josepfont@cambraben.es
W www.josepfont.com

J. Roca [85]
Passeig de Gràcia, 18
08007 Barcelona
T 93 318 32 66
Diagonal, 580
08021 Barcelona
T 93 200 07 77
W www.jroca.com

Konrad Muhr [47]
Carrer dels Sombrerers, 25
08003 Barcelona
T 93 268 31 73
E info@konradmuhr.com
W www.konradmuhr.com

Kowasa Gallery [90]
Carrer de Mallorca, 235, Bajos
08008 Barcelona
T 93 215 80 58
F 93 215 80 54
E info@kowasa.com
W www.kowasa.com

Laie [85]
Carrer de Pau Claris 85
08010 Barcelona
Llibreria:
T 93 318 17 39
Cafè:
T 93 302 73 10
F 93 412 02 50
E info@laie.es
W www.laie.es

Lailo [73]
Carrer de la Riera Baixa, 20
08001 Barcelona
T 93 441 37 49

Lliure de Gràcia [99]
Carrer del Montseny, 47
08012 Barcelona
T 93 228 97 47
F 93 424 34 53

L'Olive [87]
Carrer de Balmes, 47
08007 Barcelona
T 93 452 1990
F 93 451 24 18

Luka Home Made [38]
Carrer de la Comtessa de Sobradiel, 10
08001 Barcelona
T 93 660 610 979

Lupino [67]
Carrer del Carme, 33
08001 Barcelona
T 93 412 36 97

Luz de Gas [104]
Carrer de Muntaner, 246
08021 Barcelona
T 93 209 77 11
F 93 414 17 59
W www.luzdegas.com

Lydia Delgado [169]
Carrer de Minerva, 21
08006 Barcelona
T 93 218 16 30
F 93 218 22 25

La Manual Alpargatera [164]
Carrer d'Avinyó, 7
08002 Barcelona
T 93 301 01 72
F 93 301 18 29
E manualp@seker.es
W www.lamanualal pargatera.com

Mar Rodriguez [170]
Carrer dels Mirallers, 7, Local 1
08003 Barcelona
T 93 268 34 30
E mar@marrodriguez.com
W www.marrodriguez.com

Marsella [64]
Carrer de Sant Pau, 65
08001 Barcelona
T 93 442 72 63

La Marthe [22]
Carrer de Sant Sever, 1
08002 Barcelona
T 93 318 81 77

Mercat de la Boqueria Sant Josep [67]
La Rambla 85–89
08002 Barcelona

Mercat Encants Vells [82]
Dos de Maig, 186
(corner of Carrer de Cartagena)
08013 Barcelona
T 93 246 30 30

Mercat de Sant Antoni [74]
Comte d'Urgell, 1
08011 Barcelona

Merry Ant [156]
Carrer del Peu de la Creu, 23
08001 Barcelona

Mesopatamia [99]
Carrer de Verdi 65
08012 Barcelona
T 93 237 15 63

La Miranda del Museu [151]
Museu d'Història de Catalunya
4th floor
Plaça de Pau Vila 1
08039 Barcelona
T 93 225 47 00

Montcada • Taller [53]
Placeta de Montcada, 10 bis
08003 Barcelona
T 93 319 15 81
E espaiart@montcadataller.com
W www.montcadataller.com

Monestir de Pedralbes and Col•lecció Thyssen-Bornemisza [111]
Baixada del Monestir, 9
T 93 481 10 41/93 280 14 34
W www.museothyssen.org

Monestir i Església de Santa Anna [16]
Carrer de Santa Anna, 27–29
08002 Barcelona

La Morera [53]
Carrer del Fossar de les Moreres, 5
08003 Barcelona
T 93 315 29 60

Museu d'Art Contemporani de Barcelona (MACBA) [71]
Plaça dels Àngels, 1
08001 Barcelona
T 93 412 08 10
F 93 412 46 02
W www.macba.es

Museu de la Xocolota [54]
Plaça de Pons i Clerch
08003 Barcelona
T 93 268 78 78
F 93 268 78 79
E museu@pastisseria.com
W www.museuxocolata.com

Museu d'Historia de la Ciutat [21]
Plaça del Rei, 1
08002 Barcelona
T 93 315 11 11
F 93 315 09 57
E museuhistoria@mail.bcn.es
W www.museuhistoria.bcn.es

Museu Frederic Marès [21]
Plaça de Sant Iu, 5–6
08002 Barcelona
T 93 310 58 00
F 93 319 41 16
E museumares@mail.bcn.es

Museu Maritim [63]
Avinguda de les Drassanes
08001 Barcelona
T 93 342 99 20
F 93 318 78 76
E m.maritim@diba.es
W www.diba.es/mmaritim

Museu Nacional d'Art de Catalunya [77]
Mirador Palau Nacional, 6–10
08004 Barcelona
T 93 622 03 75
F 93 622 03 74
E mnac@mnac.es
W www.mnac.es

Museu Picasso [50]
Carrer de Montcada, 15
08003 Barcelona
T 93 319 63 10
F 93 315 01 02
E museupicasso@mail.bcn.es
W museupicasso.bcn.es

Museu Tèxtil i d'Indumentària [50]
Carrer de Montcada, 12–14
08003 Barcelona
T 93 310 45 16/93 319 76 03
F 93 310 66 46
E museutextil@mail.bcn.es
W www.museutextil.bcn.es

Muxart [165]
Carrer del Roselló, 230
08008 Barcelona
T 93 488 10 64

Nina Pawlowsky [167]
Carrer de Nou Sant Francesc, 17
08002 Barcelona
T 93 412 52 67

Octubre [104]
Carrer Julián Romea, 18
08006 Barcelona
T 93 218 25 18

On Land [171]
Carrer de la Princesa, 25
08003 Barcelona
T 93 310 02 11
Carrer de València, 273
08009 Barcelona
T 93 215 56 25
E info@on-land.com
W www.on-land.com

Ot [142]
Carrer Torres, 25
08012 Barcelona
T 93 284 77 52
E otrestaurant@hotmail.com

Otto Zutz [107]
Carrer de Lincoln, 15
08006 Barcelona
T 93 238 07 22
F 93 238 06 77
W www.ottozutz.com

Oven [57]
Carrer de Ramon Turró, 126
08005 Barcelona
T 93 221 06 02
E reservas@oven.ws
W www.oven.ws

Palau de la Música Catalana [21]
Carrer de Sant Françesc de Paula, 2
08003 Barcelona
T 93 295 72 00
F 93 295 72 10
W www.palaumusica.org

Palau Güell [63]
Carrer Nou de la Rambla, 3–5
08001 Barcelona
T 93 317 39 74

Palau Robert [93]
Centre d'Informació de Catalunya
Passeig de Gràcia, 107
08003 Barcelona
T 93 238 40 00
F 93 238 40 10
W www.gencat.net/probert

La Paloma [73]
Carrer del Tigre, 27
08001 Barcelona
T 93 301 68 97
F 93 317 72 225
E lapaloma@lapaloma-bcn.com
W www.lapaloma-bcn.com

Papers Coma [50]
Carrer de Montcada, 20
08003 Barcelona
T 93 319 76 01
W www.paperscoma.com

Parc Güell [111]
Carrer d'Olot
08024 Barcelona

Park Hotel [126]
Avinguda Marquès de l'Argentera, 11
08003 Barcelona
T 93 319 60 00
F 93 319 45 19
E parkhotel@parkhotelbarcelona.com
W www.parkhotelbarcelona.com

La Parra [74]
Carrer de Joanot Martorell, 3
08014 Barcelona
T 93 332 51 34

Passadís del Pep [130]
Plaça del Palau, 2
08003 Barcelona
T 93 310 10 21
F 93 319 60 56
E restaurant@passadis.com
W www.passadis.com

Pavelló Barcelona/Pavelló Mies van der Rohe [77]
Avinguda del Marquès de Comillas
T 93 423 40 16
F 93 426 37 72
E pavello@miesbcn.com
W www.miesbcn.com

Pinotxo [67]
La Boqueria, 66
La Rambla, 91
08002 Barcelona
T 93 317 17 31

Pipa Club [30]
Plaça Reial, 3,
08002 Barcelona
T 93 302 47 32/93 301 11 65
E bpipaclub@hotmail.com
W www.bpipaclub.com

Pitín Bar [152]
Passeig del Born, 34
08003 Barcelona
T/F 93 319 50 87
E pitinbar@mx2.redestb.es

Plastic Bar [152]
Passeig del Born, 19
08003 Barcelona

Pou Dolç [34]
Baixada de Sant Miquel, 6
08002 Barcelona
T 93 412 05 79

Principal (El Principal del Tragaluz) [133]
Carrer de Provença, 286–288
08008 Barcelona
T 93 272 08 45
F 93 272 08 47

Els Quatre Gats [16]
Carrer de Montsío, 3 bis
08002 Barcelona
T 93 302 41 40
F 93 317 40 33
W www.4gats.com

Quimet i Quimet [63]
Carrer del Poeta Cabanyes, 25
08004 Barcelona
T 93 442 31 42

El Racó d'en Freixa [145]
Carrer de Sant Elíes, 22
08006 Barcelona
T 93 209 75 59
F 93 209 79 18

Rafa Teja Atelier [162]
Carrer de Santa Maria, 18
08003 Barcelona
T 93 310 27 85
F 93 289 28 05

Raimon Ollé [107]
Carrer de Santaló 39–41
08021 Barcelona
T 93 200 45 80

El Rancho Grande [137]
Avinguda Diagonal, 73
08019 Barcelona
T 93 307 07 05

Ras [68]
Carrer del Doctor Dou, 10
08001 Barcelona
T 93 412 71 99
E ras@oike.com
W www.actar.es/ras.html

Restaurant Barceloneta [54]
L'Escar, 22
Moll dels Pescadors – Port Vell
08039 Barcelona
T/F 93 221 21 11

Restaurant Plaça dels Àngels [73]
Carrer Ferlandina 23
08001 Barcelona
T 93 329 40 47

Roig Robi [144]
Carrer de Séneca 20
08006 Barcelona
T 93 218 92 22/93 217 97 38
F 93 415 78 42
W www.roigrobi.com

Roser i Francesc [88]
Carrer València, 285
08009 Barcelona
T 93 459 14 53

Sala Exposicions La Capella [64]
Antic Hospital Santa Creu
Carrer de l'Hospital, 56
08001 Barcelona
T 93 442 71 71

Salero [53]
Carrer del Rec 60
08003 Barcelona
T 93 319 80 22

Salsitas [158]
Carrer Nou de la Rambla, 22
08001 Barcelona
T 268 74 30

Salterio [22]
Carrer Sant Domènec del Call, 4
08002 Barcelona
T 93 302 5028

Sandwich and Friends [53]
Passeig del Born, 27
08003 Barcelona
T 93 310 07 86

Santa Maria [140]
Carrer del Comerç, 17
08003 Barcelona
T 93 315 12 27

Semon [107]
Carrer de Ganduxer, 31
08021 Barcelona
Carrer de Santa Fe
de Nou Mèxic, 25
08021 Barcelona
T 93 201 55 07

Semproniana [89]
Carrer del Rosselló, 148
08036 Barcelona
T 93 453 18 20

Senyor Parellada [45]
Carrer de l'Argenteria, 37
08003 Barcelona
T 93 310 50 94

7 Portes [57]
Passeig de Isabel II, 14
08003 Barcelona
T 93 319 30 33/93 319 29 50
F 93 319 30 46
E admon@setportes.com
W www.7portes.com

Silenus [70]
Carrer Àngels, 8
08001 Barcelona
T/F 93 302 26 80
E cob@arrakis.es

Sita Murt [33]
Carrer d'Avinyó, 18
08002 Barcelona
T 93 301 00 06

Slokai [34]
Carrer del Palau, 5
08002 Barcelona
T 93 317 90 94

So_Da [33]
Carrer d'Avinyó, 24
08002 Barcelona
T 93 412 27 76

Subirà Cereria [21]
Baixada de la Llibreteria, 7
08002 Barcelona
T 93 315 26 26

Taverna El Glop [99]
Carrer de Montmany 46
08012 Barcelona
T 93 213 70 58

Taxidermista [30]
Plaça Reial, 8
08002 Barcelona
T 93 412 45 36

Teatre Nacional de Catalunya [82]
Plaça de les Arts 1
08013 Barcelona
T 93 306 57 20
W www.tnc.es

Tetería Jazmín [100]
Carrer de Maspons, 11
08012 Barcelona
T 93 218 71 84

Tèxtil Café [49]
Museu de Tèxtil i Indumentària
Carrer de Montcada, 12
08003 Barcelona
T 93 268 25 98

Torre d'Alta Mar [143]
Passeig Joan de Borbó 88
08039 Barcelona
T 93 221 00 07
W www.torredealtamar.com

Tortillería Flash-Flash [104]
Carrer de la Granada
del Penedès, 25
08006 Barcelona
T 93 237 09 90

Tragaluz & Tragrapid [90]
Passatge de la Concepció, 5
08008 Barcelona
T 93 487 06 21/93 487 01 96

Tresserra [108]
Carrer de Josep Bertrand, 17
08021 Barcelona
T 93 200 49 22
F 93 200 47 34
E collection@tresserra.com
W www.tresserra.com

Va de Vi [46]
Carrer de Banys Vells, 16
08003 Barcelona
T 93 319 29 00

Valentina [37]
Plaça de Régomir, 2
08002 Barcelona
T 93 310 79 21

El Vaso de Oro [159]
Carrer de Balboa, 6
08003 Barcelona
T 93 319 30 98

La Venta [131]
Plaça del Doctor Andreu
08035 Barcelona
T 93 212 64 55

Vila Viniteca [173]
Carrer dels Agullers, 7
08003 Barcelona
T 93 268 32 27
F 93 268 31 59
E info@vilaviniteca.es
W www.vilaviniteca.es

Vinçon [90]
Passeig de Gràcia 96
(entrances also at Provença 273 and Paul Claris, 175/179)
08008 Barcelona
T 93 215 60 50
F 93 215 50 37
E bcn@vincon.com
W www.vincon.com

La Vinya del Senyor [151]
Plaça de Santa Maria, 5
08003 Barcelona
T 93 310 33 79

wah wah [73]
Carrer de la Riera Baixa, 14
08001 Barcelona
T 93 442 37 03
F 93 442 23 25
E wah-wah@mx3.redestb.es

Walden 8 [108]
Avinguda de la Indústria, 12
Sant Just Desvern, Barcelona
T 93 499 03 42
W www.elmirador.org

El Xampanyet [49]
Carrer de Montcada, 22
08003 Barcelona
T 93 319 70 03

Xiringuita Escribà [57]
Litoral Mar, 42 (Platja
del Bogatell)
08005 Barcelona
T 93 221 07 29

Xocoa [174]
Carrer d'En Bot 4
08002 Barcelona
T 93 318 89 91
F 93 846 15 48
Carrer de Petritxol 11
08002 Barcelona
T 93 301 11 97
E info@xocoa.com

Xurreria Trebol [99]
Carrer de Córsega 341
08037 Barcelona
T 93 217 95 94

Zero [73]
Carrer de la Riera Baixa, 12
08001 Barcelona
T 93 441 01 94
W www.zerobcn.com

[Z]INK [33]
Carrer d'Avinyó, 14
08002 Barcelona
T 93 342 62 88

Zsu Zsa [33]
Carrer d'Avinyó, 50
08002 Barcelona
T 93 412 49 65

MONTSENY

By car, take the A-7 autopista about 50 kilometres to Sant Celoni, exit 11, then another 30 kilometres to the hotel in Sant Marçal. To enter the Parc Natural de Montseny, take a trail for Turo de l'Home from the Sant Celoni road, or take the BV301 to Figueró, where there is a Tagamanent mountain trail starting off the train station. Ask at the hotel for El Racó de Can Fabes, a few minutes drive into Sant Celoni: it's behind the town hall.

Sant Marçal
Hotel Monestir
Ctra. Sant Celoni a Sant Marçal
Km. 28 Montseny
08460 Viladrau
T/F 93 847 30 43
E reservas@hotelsantmarcal.com
W www.hotelsantmarcal.com
Rooms from €120

El Racó de Can Fabes
Sant Joan, 6
08470 Sant Celoni
T 93 867 28 51
F 93 867 38 61
W www.racocanfabes.com

FIGUERAS AND ENVIRONS

By car, take the A7/E15 to Figueres, past Girona. The Teatre Museu is in the Figueres city centre. For the Cadaqués house in Portlligat and El Bulli, take the C-260 road from the A-7. Before you enter the town of Roses, a small road to the left takes you to Cadaqués and another road to the left takes you up to Portlligat, the small house-musuem. You'll know it by the two broken heads surmounting the wall. For the Castell Gala in Púbol, head off the N-11 north of Girona onto the C-255 to La Bisbal, Púbol village is on this road. To reach the Hotel Mas Falgarona, from the A7/E15 take the N260 toward Avinyonet. Go through the town to a small road that branches left.

Teatre Museu Dalí
Plaça Gala-Salvador Dalí, 5
Figueres
T 972 677 500
E t-mgrups@dali-estate.org
W www.salvador-dali.org/eng.fmuseus.htm

Salvador Dalí Museum House
Portlligat
Cadaqués
T 972 677 500
E pllgrups@dali-estate.org
W www.salvador-dali.org/eng.fmuseus.htm
Prior booking is essential and can be done by telephone, fax or email. On the day of the visit, the ticket must be picked up half-an-hour before entering. Open from 15 March to 6 January

Casa-Museu Castell Gala Dalí
Púbol
17120 La Pera
T 972 488 655
E pbgrups@dali-estate.org
W www.salvador-dali.org/eng.fmuseus.htm
Open from 15 March to 1 November (rest of year, group visits by prior booking)

Hotel Mas Falgarona
Avinyonet de Puigventós
17742 Girona
T 972 546 628
F 972 547 071
E email@masfalgarona.com
W www.masfalgarona.com
Rooms from €200

El Bulli
Cala Montjoi
Ap. 3D
17480 Roses
Girona
T 972 150 457
F 972 150 717
E bulli@elbulli.com
W www.elbulli.com
From April to June, dinner only, from 8 p.m; closed Sundays and Mondays. From July to September, open every day for dinner only, from 8 p.m. Closed October to March.

CARDONA

Located on a hill opposite the town of Cardona, the parador is 85 kilometres from Barcelona by car. Take the E9/C16 to Manresa, then the A-18 motorway (or C-55), leaving Manresa towards Solsona.

Parador de Cardona
8261 Cardona
T 93 869 12 75
F 93 869 16 36
E cardona@parador.es
W www.parador.es
Rooms from €120

SITGES AND ALT PENEDÈS

From Barcelona by car take the C-32 motorway south toward Tarragona and follow signs to Sitges, about 35 kilometres. Leaving from Barcelona, Vilafranca del Penedès and Sant Sadurní d'Anoia are both located off the C-15 from the A-7, which runs south; from Sitges you'll need to travel inland to the A-7 by way of the C-32 motorway (which connects with the A7 farther south) or on smaller local roads. The Bodegues Torres visitors' centre is outside the town of Vilafranca, near Pacs del Penedès, on the BP2121 in the direction of Sant Martí Sarroca.

Hotel El Xalet
Illa de Cuba, 35
08870 Sitges
T 93 811 00 70
F 93 894 55 79
Rooms from €100

Museu de Vi
Pl. Jaume I, 1
08720 Vilafranca del Penedès
T 93 890 05 82
F 93 817 00 36

Bodegues Torres
Miguel Torres S.A.
Finca El Maset s/nº
08739 Pacs del Penedès
T 93 817 74 87

Caves Codorniu
Avda Codorniu
Sant Sadurní d'Anoia
T 93 818 32 32
W www.codorniu.es